LIVE! FROM DEATH VALLEY

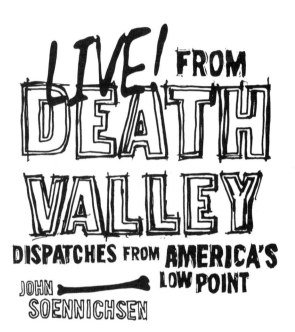

LIVE! FROM DEATH VALLEY

DISPATCHES FROM AMERICA'S LOW POINT

JOHN SOENNICHSEN

SASQUATCH BOOKS
SEATTLE

Printed in Canada
Published by Sasquatch Books
Distributed by Publishers Group West
15 14 13 12 11 10 09 08 07 06 05   8 7 6 5 4 3 2 1

Cover photograph by Arthur Rothstein/Corbis
Interior photographs and map by John Soennichsen
Design by Stewart A. Williams

Library of Congress Cataloging-in-Publication Data
Soennichsen, John Robert.
        Live from Death Valley : dispatches from America's low point / John
Soennichsen.
        p.cm.
Includes biographical references.
ISBN 1-57061-448-2
   1. Death Valley (Calif. and Nev.)—Description and travel. 2. Soennichsen, John
Robert—Travel—Death Valley (Calif. and Nev.) 3. Natural history—Death Valley
(Calif. and Nev.) 4. Death Valley (Calif. and Nev.)—History. I. Title.

F868.D2S64 2005
917.94'8704'54—dc22   2005042561

Sasquatch Books
119 South Main Street, Suite 400
Seattle, WA 98104
(206) 467-4300
www.sasquatchbooks.com
custserv@sasquatchbooks.com

To my mother and father, who sparked my love of hands-on encounters with nature, and who not only accepted but encouraged my insatiable need for independence and occasional solitary journeys to the middle of nowhere.

To my loving wife and children, who have patiently endured my regularly scheduled episodes of staring off into space, and who continue to provide the support and encouragement I need as a writer.

Lastly, thanks to all those wonderful and inspiring people I have met along the way. You all know who you are.

CONTENTS

AUTHOR'S NOTE

Dozens of human beings, alive and dead, managed to find their way into this book. Many are historical figures who are worthy of honor, or at least deserve to be mentioned by name. Many other people, however, are still very much alive and, for whatever reasons, may not want their real names used in these pages. Out of respect for their privacy, I have therefore fictionalized many of the names in this book. —*J. S.*

INTRODUCTION

The ancient Shoshones called it *Tomesha*—Ground on Fire. In 1891, writer John Spears described it as "gray and sombre; desolate and forbidding." To Arthur Burdick, writing in 1904, it was a "great drug warehouse" in which "the passing winds whirl clouds of poisonous dust through the air." Even Edward Abbey, who spent his life penning eloquent prose about the beauty of the American desert, once referred to Death Valley as "dead, dead, deathly."

So why have I come to love this parched, superheated, desolate, and dusty corner of the world? Is it mere bullheadedness, a cynical desire to cherish something that most would be inclined to despise? I suspect it's more than that. I think my love affair with Death Valley began when I first experienced the vehement honesty of this place; when I first discovered that Death Valley did not seek to hide its appearance with vegetative cosmetics, did not adorn itself in soft and sumptuous outer garments or employ subtly filtered lighting or cool ocean breezes to tempt my senses. And it never tried to seduce me with splashing streams and lacy ferns and moss-covered trails through cool forest glens.

Perhaps my lifelong obsession with this place is really an unhealthy fascination. Maybe I am drawn to Death Valley because of the way it bares itself almost pornographically, exciting the senses with its wide-open frankness, the take-it-or-leave-it exposition of its geologic anatomy that drew me to it at the impressionable age of thirteen.

There is a bitter, almost corrosive quality to the deep desert trench that is Death Valley. A view of its saline floor from Aguereberry Point is to the eyes what smelling salts are to the olfactory system—abruptly awakening, harsh and unforgiving. Once down in the chasm itself, the stinging heat is grating on the skin. Just getting around presents challenges. Spires of razor-edged salt, ragged volcanic rocks, and the pointed thorns of cactus and cockleburs can pierce your skin and heighten the sensation that you are being tested in this place. The smell of its water is acrid. Its taste approaches nauseating. The very feel of the air is styptic.

Even history here is raw. The earliest white men arrived by accident, then spent the next few months trying their damnedest to get out. Subsequent residents—miners and malcontents, showmen and shamans—were either unwilling outcasts from civilized society or avid seekers of solitude. Most tales of human endeavor in this place conclude with someone's demise.

Today, nearly a million tourists visit Death Valley each year, coming and going along the 300 miles of paved roads in this 5,264-square-mile national park. There are gas stations here, convenience stores, a visitor center, and four-star hotel. But close by are places that don't see a living soul for years at a time. And despite the modern conveniences, it's quite easy to die here; more than two hundred people have done so over the past 150 years.

During a period of nearly two decades, I took trips to the region to hike and explore as much of its forbidding desert landscape as possible. Sometimes I was accompanied by friends from the Los Angeles area and from Oregon. In later years my wife came with me. But most often, I traveled alone.

This book is my attempt to capture in words my reverence for Death Valley's geology, history, and harsh environment. It is a reverence conceived in naiveté, nourished through repeated exploration, and polished with the passage of time. It is the story of how this region helped construct my views on the environment, tourism, solitude, and religion, among other topics. It is part memoir and part adventure tale; part history lesson and part coming-of-age story.

More than anything, it is my final love letter to an ill-tempered yet incredibly candid mistress—a mistress who still calls to me now and again whenever the summer sun blisters my face, when a stiff breeze blows sand in my eyes, or when white stars glimmer in a black sky.

Valley of the Shadow

CHRISTMAS DAY, 1849. A lone man in ragged clothes picks his way along the rock-strewn floor of a narrow desert canyon. For two days, twenty-eight-year-old William Lewis Manly has followed the twisting passage as it probes the black core of a brooding volcanic range. Too numb to ache any longer, his legs propel him along mechanically, one foot after the other. His mind is no longer conscious of the steps he takes; it dwells instead on the shadowy figures of those he left behind. He sees the haggard faces of the men, their flesh red with sun, their lips grimly sealed as if by some invisible clamp. He sees the women in their tattered frocks, their limbs a patchwork of bites and scratches. And he sees the children's tender faces suddenly aged, their listless eyes gazing blankly.

Quite abruptly, Manly comes upon a place where the canyon floor descends steeply. Here his legs buckle under him and he throws out both arms to break his fall. Hitting the ground hard, he winces in pain as shards of rock pierce the flesh of both palms. Then he pulls himself to his feet, pauses a moment to stare at the blood on his hands, and moves on.

———※———

Fifty-one days earlier, on November 4, 1849, Manly's small band of California-bound emigrants—called the Bennett-Arcane party—had broken from the Sand Walking Company, a well-organized wagon train, to follow an uncertain shortcut to the goldfields. They carried with them a copy of a hand-drawn map showing a route west that they hoped would pass through hills of lush grass and plentiful water all the way to the Sierras. But just four weeks into the cutoff, the party found itself rolling through a waterless and increasingly barren landscape. About this time, a group of single men who called themselves Jayhawkers moved ahead of the others, claiming that women and children would only slow them down. The men, women, and children who remained continued southwest. But eight weeks of aimless wandering only drew them deeper into an arid wasteland of sharp-edged mountain peaks and lifeless saline basins.

Finally their weathered wagons creaked to a halt before a black-walled chain of mountains running north and south. Here their outlook brightened briefly. Surely, they thought, this was the last range of mountains separating them from the fertile valleys of California. But long days of travel had left them exhausted. Two children were sick and five oxen were near death for lack of grass and water. Because there was a faint little spring here, Manly suggested that the others rest and regain their strength while he scouted ahead. His plan was to map out a trail, then return and guide them through the maze of cliffs to safety.

After two days of hiking, Manly spies the peak of a distant snow-covered mountain just visible above a canyon wall ahead. It is the same peak that he and his party have spotted on and off for weeks. His cracked lips part in a faint smile as he hears a flock of geese overhead. It is a good omen; he now believes that Owens Lake, a wintering spot for migrating birds, must surely lie ahead.

Not long after, Manly rounds a bend in the narrow canyon and feels a rush of warm air. A funnel of sand whirls around him as he pauses to shift the weight of the pack on his back. Then he continues down the widening passage. Two more turns and the canyon wash abruptly spits him onto the gravelly apron of a sloping alluvial fan. From this windblown height, Manly commands a disturbing view of a landscape he will never forget.

Before him lies a deep gash in the ground, a running scar so bleak and oppressive that he drops to his knees and begins to weep. To the north, some fifty miles or more, the floor of this mammoth ditch rises slightly in elevation; to the south, the land falls away and there appears to be a body of water. But as he knows well from previous disappointments, this is no freshwater lake. Lifeless in appearance, its steely gray water is fringed with a froth of brine.

Manly now directs his gaze across the sinkhole toward the base of the lofty, snow-covered mountain. Is this peak part of the Sierra Nevada, or does it belong to another range, another barrier to be crossed? The bottom of the peak lies south of where he stands, across the width of this lifeless trench—fifteen, perhaps twenty, miles away. Manly can tell it is miles from base to peak; there is no practical way to reach the deep snow and thin stands of timber on the mountain's topmost crags.

Dropping his gaze to the saline gulch below, Manly scans the shimmering flats for signs of grass or trees or game. He sees none of these in any direction, only sand and salt and rock and brine. As he stands upon the sloping apron of debris, poised at the edge of the most lifeless and desolate piece of land in the universe, it occurs to him that he has arrived at the gateway to hell.

CHAPTER ONE

—✳—

BAPTISM OF FIRE

There is always one moment in childhood when the door opens and lets the future in.

—GRAHAM GREENE,
The Power and the Glory, 1940

When William Lewis Manly first viewed Death Valley from Furnace Creek Wash, he surely must have experienced a phenomenal sense of sorrow and disbelief. My own introduction to the place was with a supreme lack of interest. It was 1965 and I was thirteen years old, the youngest member of a typical middle-class family living in a painfully ordinary Southern California subdivision.

The Jarvis family had come for Sunday dinner. As the adults gathered in the dining room and the four of us kids scrunched

1

around a small kitchen table, I overheard Stan Jarvis suddenly propose from the other room that the whole lot of us spend Christmas vacation together. I remember straining to hear as he talked about a stark desert landscape some two hundred miles northeast of Los Angeles, a place beyond the edge of nowhere called Death Valley.

On that warm summer evening, my first reaction to his idea was simple apathy. The only thing I knew about Death Valley was that an actor named Ronald Reagan hung out there a lot. I saw no reason to learn any more about the place. I also knew if I was dragged out into some dusty desert sinkhole, I'd miss out on one full week of fun with my friends. No visits to the local swimming pool. No rock fights in the vacant lot behind the high school. No evenings spent in the balcony of the Fox Theater, lobbing handfuls of popcorn into the darkness below.

Fortunately I soon forgot about these winter plans and spent the remainder of that summer savoring the fellowship of flag football, the camaraderie of a good wrestling match, and the awakening of competitive spirit as we sped on our bikes down long rows of withering orange trees.

It was a fine time in our lives. Our strength and agility were at a peak, our common sense as yet undeveloped. We were old enough to spend our days unfettered by parental supervision but too young to worry about the gritty images of reality dancing across our TV screens each night. And so we devoured each day with insatiable hunger, riding our bikes down a thousand nameless trails through a private wilderness of hills and gullies, clearings and creek beds; rushing through the years of our youth as though, if we only pedaled fast enough, we might escape adulthood altogether.

Sooner than we wanted, the summer came crashing to a close and we headed back to school. Fall quickly gave way to winter, and the long-awaited first day of Christmas vacation was upon us. On that very day of liberation, filled with misgivings, my sister and I were strapped into the back seat of our family's '62 Impala and carried away from the secure little piece of suburbia we knew so well.

Far out into the wild nothingness of the Mojave Desert we drove. North along the eastern flank of the Sierras, past the briny dregs of Searles Lake and the sulfurous stink of a town called Trona, down into the arid Panamint Valley, up again into the rocky Panamint Mountains, then down, down, down the final, ear-popping descent from six thousand feet in elevation to a point more than a hundred feet below sea level.

Into the valley of death rode the '62 Chevy. Land's end. Everyone out. Abandon all hope, ye who enter.

CHAPTER TWO

STRANGER THAN FICTION

Death Valley has been rightly named. In this great drug warehouse arise deadly vapors, and the passing winds whirl clouds of poisonous dust through the air, when, if inhaled, will eat the vitals and eventually rob one of life.

—Arthur J. Burdick,
The Mystic Mid-Region: The Deserts of the Southwest, 1904

Despite Arthur Burdick's warning, Death Valley's air is no more poisonous than that of any other desert place. Still, his melodramatics are understandable; Death Valley is well-suited to the stretching of truth.

Why? Because the whole region is already chock-full of bizarre *realities*. This is a place where alternating beds of salt and gravel descend a thousand feet below the surface; where inch-long fish frolic in 112-degree saltwater; where two-hundred-pound boulders slide mysteriously across a dry lake bed, leaving tracks a hundred feet long. And if we are willing to believe in realities such as these, why not also believe in Burdick's whirling clouds of poisonous vapors?

For that matter, why not believe all the other wild tales that Death Valley has engendered over more than a century. Stories about waves of sand that rush upon men and swallow them whole. Cliffs of solid silver and dry riverbeds littered with gold. Creeks that flow with arsenic. Lost civilizations and underground caverns.

So where is this bizarre and frightening place? Death Valley lies in the extreme northeastern part of California's Mojave Desert, sidling up alongside the border with southwestern Nevada. The major feature is the valley itself, which is actually a large desert graben, or fault-formed trough, flanked by high mountains. This deep furrow in the ground is about 130 miles long and from 5 to 15 miles across. A great deal more land is included within the park's boundaries, however. At more than 50 miles wide and 150 miles long, it is the largest U.S. national park outside Alaska.

The west-side mountain ranges—collectively called the Panamints—do an effective job of blocking the already low amounts of moisture that manage to cross the Sierras. This accounts for the extremely dry climate of Death Valley, where humidity—rarely rising above 10 percent in the summer—sometimes drops to near zero. On the east is the Amargosa Range, made up of the Black, Funeral, and Grapevine Mountains. At the southern border of the park are the Owlshead Mountains; the Sylvania Mountains enclose it on the north.

Except for the highway entering from the south—and this is the least traveled entrance route to Death Valley—every access point features a dramatic drop in elevation over a very short period of time and distance. Once over a mountain pass, you drop, drop, drop, your ears pop, and you sense you are descending to the center of the earth. Well, to sea level anyway. The entire valley floor is at sea level or below.

The close proximity of high and low points makes for Death Valley's striking appearance as an incredibly deep place. The lowest point in the western hemisphere is here—282 feet below sea level near Badwater. Towering over this point is Telescope Peak, at just over 11,000 feet.

Death Valley may be best known for its extreme summer temperatures. Temperatures of 120 degrees Fahrenheit and above are common between June and September. Why is this place so hot? Death Valley's depth and shape are partly to blame. It is a long, narrow graben with most of its floor below sea level. But it is flanked by high mountain ranges that trap heat in the valley's depths. Even when the sun sets during summer months, there is little relief, with lows dropping only to the 90s and low 100s. And while it is true that heated air rises and then falls in a cooler state, falling air in Death Valley is compressed and heated even more by the high air pressure of the valley's lowest elevations. These moving masses of superheated air then blow through the valley and create even higher temperatures.

The record air temperature here topped out at 134, and even that number—recorded in 1913—is probably conservative, since it wasn't taken at the lowest and hottest point in the park. Oddly enough, that same year also saw the coldest reading ever at Death Valley, 15 degrees in January. And 1913 was a wet year, with 4.54 inches of rain (the annual average is just below 2 inches). Despite these extremes, however, the weather is so warm and inviting in spring and fall that hundreds of thousands of visitors are attracted from frigid northern climates to bask in the 70- and 80-degree sunshine.

※ ※ ※ ※ ※

Death Valley's reputation—indeed its very name—will always be linked to the frightful experiences of the '49ers who crossed its saline floor. They were the first white people to cross it, and one or more members of their party named it before they departed. Yet the real story behind its creation is devoid of human impact. Death Valley's autobiography is a tale of grabens and fault lines, receding seas and folding escarpments. The main characters are rocks, sand, air, and water. The setting is a land form conceived millions of years ago.

To understand how this place came to look the way it does today, we must first gaze back to an age when there was no valley at all—a time long before the earth's crust began to twist and stretch, fault and fold; long before blocks of mountains were thrown up and valleys began to sink. In the Paleozoic era (300 to 500 million years ago), the region was largely covered by an ocean. The creatures just offshore were neither fish nor reptile, but were poised at some schizophrenic state between the two. Layers of bone fragments that littered the ocean bed would later form the limestone found in many parts of Death Valley. As time passed and oceans receded, the only mammals to be found were still undeveloped balls of fluff.

Moving ahead to a point some 135 million years ago, events began to occur that would determine the shape of the great trench to come. The sea withdrew and a massive mountain range appeared in a dramatic upthrust of volcanic rock, then promptly wore away until it was gone.

This brings us to a significant age of change for the region, the Cenozoic, which began some 65 million years ago. This era initially gave the region low mountains and broad plains. Tall grasses and lush vegetation covered higher ground while valleys were crossed by shallow streams and dotted with lakes. But this idyllic landscape had been painted on a moving canvas, an unstable terrain of abrupt and continual change. Fickle climatic variations turned verdant valleys to saline deserts, then back to lush grassland, over hundreds of thousands of years.

At this same time, and continuing to perhaps less than 100,000 years ago, huge faults formed in the earth's crust, followed by dramatic folding and volcanic eruptions that lifted mountains and lowered valleys. The original floor of Death

Valley was eight thousand to ten thousand feet lower than it is now. Subsequent periods of erosion and filling of the valley with debris raised the floor to its present elevation.

Water, though seemingly absent in the Death Valley region, was present in great volumes some 120,000 to 180,000 years ago. Both Death Valley and its neighbor, Panamint Valley, held huge lakes, perhaps five hundred or six hundred feet deep. And the bulk of the region's most recognizable geologic features were being formed by water. At Zabriskie Point, for example, the badlands we see today were developed on a foundation of mudstone, a type of soft rock formed by the depositing of silt and clay in a prehistoric lake, then compressed and cemented together.

The final transition to saline desert and a landscape as we see it today occurred over the past several thousand years. Lake Manly had evaporated earlier, but the surface of Death Valley was still covered by a salty lake perhaps thirty feet deep. As the climate warmed and rainfall decreased, the lake slowly evaporated and minerals in the water became more dense. Finally only a layer of muck remained and salts began to crystallize, leaving deposits a thousand feet deep.

Trees and shrubs of a temperate nature withered and died, to be replaced by vegetation tolerant of salt, sand, and heat. Most warm-blooded creatures moved higher into the mountains surrounding the now barren valley, or graben, between the Panamint and Funeral ranges. Then the whole place sat and waited a few thousand years, probably looking much as it does today. Even so, erosion from infrequent but violent storm runoff can dramatically alter in just a few hundred years what took millions of years to form; thus we will never know *exactly* what Death Valley was like as little as a thousand years ago, let alone a million.

<hr />

And what of the region's human history? If the earth's geologic record could be said to occupy twenty-four hours, the entire history of humans would take about four seconds. It was not until some point after the last dinosaurs became fossils and the first modern mammals evolved that our ancestors appeared on earth. This was probably about three million years ago, a short yawn in geologic time.

Despite their successful evolution into thinking beings who eventually peopled the earth, these early humans lacked the higher levels of intelligence their descendants would one day possess—descendants like the rough-hewn frontiersmen who would throw together sheet-metal shacks and raucous saloons and brothels draped with crimson velvet and call them cities; men who would spend each day scuttling about the rocks and canyons to carve deep gashes in the earth and pull out chunks of yellow and gray metal for investing in whiskey and whores each evening.

Death Valley's earliest inhabitants—the Nevares Spring people—arrived some nine thousand years ago, and though they did not set out to build cities or roads or convenience stores, they were our cultural ancestors as surely as the Europeans, Africans, Asians, and Latinos from whose loins we would later spring. Garbed in diverse wardrobes of evolutionary development, these resourceful men and women inhabited the region for thousands of years. Only as the last global climate shifts began to leave certain parts of the world high and dry (or low and dry, in the case of Death Valley) did their tribes begin to leave these parts.

Soon—by the evolutionary calendar—the region was only sparsely inhabited by small groups that would later come to be known as the Paiutes and the Shoshone. For centuries these tenacious bands of Native Americans survived on chuckwalla lizards, mule deer, the seeds of nut pine and mesquite, and a surprising variety of gourds and melons grown in the shadowy canyons above the valley.

That's right, these folks actually thrived in Death Valley without tanning lotion, swimming pools, air conditioning, engine coolant, or ice chests. Rather than fight the elements of nature like the white men who would later occupy the floor of the stifling sinkhole year-round, these native people departed each summer for higher ground. In their absence the saline trench shimmered in waves of heat, and the land baked at ground temperatures exceeding 190 degrees.

In this fashion for hundreds of years, the cycle of seasons rotated like a wagon wheel and the land waited patiently for William Lewis Manly to stumble down Furnace Creek Wash in December of 1849, cast his eyes upon the great dry gash in the ground, and promptly proclaim it worthless.

Hell on Earth

AS WILLIAM LEWIS MANLY GAZES down at the terrifying landscape before him, he is overcome by the urge to retch. His first thought is to turn away from the scene, to retrace his steps, to tell the others that no passage exists through the black range of mountains. All this he would do were it not for that odd, undisciplined need we all have to stare in hypnotic wonder at pictures of death, at deformities of the human body, at the monumental mistakes of man and nature.

For this reason, Manly is unable to withdraw from the scene or even to turn his head. But he is able to think, to reason. And what he reasons now is that he and the others have no choice but to cross this vast sink if they are to continue west.

When he has seen enough, he drops his eyes to the ground and begins to pray for guidance. Then, in the rocky soil at his feet, he spots a set of faint footprints—three, maybe four of them trailing down the alluvial fan, then veering off to the north. Farther down the wash he finds the tracks of wagon wheels. Manly now recalls the Jayhawkers, the group of men who struck out ahead of the others nearly a month earlier. Clearly, they have come this way—passing through the same canyon he explored, then down the sloping fan of rocks and sand to enter the open wound in the earth below. Before returning to his own party, Manly decides to follow the Jayhawkers' footprints. Perhaps they have discovered a way out of the deep trench. Maybe they will leave him with some hopeful news to bring back to the others.

His plan determined, Manly stumbles down the sweeping slope of rock and debris and follows the wash out onto the valley floor. With each foot he loses in elevation, the temperature rises; when he at last reaches the floor of the sink, he stops for a moment to stare at what appears to be a moving landscape, its surface rising and falling with the waves of heat that hover just above its surface.

Encountering a rocky stretch of ground, Manly loses sight of the Jayhawkers' footprints. Thinking they have crossed to the west side of the valley, he starts across the rocky floor, hoping to pick up the trail on the other side. He hasn't traveled far before his way is impeded by a sea of jagged spikes thrusting out of the earth as high as three feet in places. The farther west he walks, the taller these spires become. By the time he reaches the midpoint of the valley, the sharp-edged pinnacles have become nearly transparent. He now realizes they are made of salt.

Clambering over these ragged spires, he comes upon a half-dozen pools of bright green water, pools that appear to drop on down to the center of the earth. Just below the surface, dense clusters of square-edged crystals cling to the lips of the pools. When Manly dips his fingers in the water and touches them to his tongue, he tastes the saltiest brine he has ever known. Moments after wetting them, his fingers are dry again and a powdery white residue coats the skin.

At this point Manly decides he will do himself better service by leaving these beds of salt and heading north along the base of the mountains. Clearly, the Jayhawkers couldn't have taken their wagons this way. He retraces his steps through the spires of salt and back to the mouth of the canyon wash. After a brief search in both directions, he picks up a faint trail heading north. Following this path some eight or nine miles north, he spots the Jayhawkers' encampment. The sky has grown dark and a cooling breeze has picked up.

Drawing nearer their camp, he spies the men—fifteen in all. Most stand about the small clearing in groups of two and three; a few hunch over a fire in the center of the encampment. A short distance away are the Jayhawkers' four remaining wagons. Stripped of their canvas covers and emptied of their contents, they look like the skeletons of large animals that have been slaughtered, gutted, and abandoned in the desert sand.

Two of the Jayhawkers' oxen have died or been shot, Manly can't tell which. Their shrunken bodies repose in the sand, stiff legs extended, eye sockets crawling with large, blue-bodied flies. A third beast has been butchered; its carcass lies in segments near the others. Draped over a nearby boulder, strips of stringy meat hang to dry. They too are alive with flies and gnats. Three other oxen are still breathing, but just barely. They huddle together like statues beside the carcasses of the wagons they pulled for so many miles.

As Manly enters the Jayhawker camp, the men welcome him warmly, though their sarcasm is as bitter as the alkali soil beneath their feet.

"The water's brackish, there's no grass, there's rocks for your pillow and sand for your blanket," says Tom McGrew as Manly approaches. "But you're more'n welcome to share it all with us."

Dropping his pack on the ground, Manly squats down beside Captain Edward Doty. He now sees that the fuel for the campfire consists of wagon parts, among them a broken wheel. Resting atop a stone in the center of the fire, the wheel spins slowly as the coals heat up beneath it. A few dozen yards away, a second campfire has been prepared to cook the meat from the slaughtered ox.

"We leave tomorrow," says Doty, gingerly plucking a burning ember from his pant leg and tossing it back into the flames. "We'll cook the meat from one ox tonight, and dry the rest to divide among us."

"Did they die for lack of grass?" asks Manly.

"Shot," says Doty. "We chose the ones that couldn't make it over the mountains. We'll tether the other three and haul 'em along with us for food."

"So . . . you've found a pass to the west?" Manly asks.

Doty laughs.

"There ain't no pass, just a spot that's a mite lower than the rest of the range. But no wagons can get over it, so we aim to hike farther north and try another way out on foot."

Tom Shannon comes over and sits down next to Manly. His face is devoid of emotion, and Manly shifts uncomfortably as the man stares at him for some time without talking.

"It's the creator's dumping ground," mutters Shannon after several minutes of silence.

"Pardon me?" says Manly.

"The place where God left the worthless dregs after creating the world."

Doty manages a brief smile.

"I like Bill Robinson's version better," he says. "Old Bill says this is the spot where Lot's wife was turned to salt, and the pillar's been broken up by the devil and spread all around the countryside. Which tale you like best, Lewis?"

Manly looks at Doty a long time, sizing up the man's state of mind.

"Both images paint a gloomy picture," he says at last. "I'd rather not choose either premise for the time being."

"Ah, we have a fence-sitter in our midst," laughs Doty, "a man unwilling to take a stand! Tell you what," he continues, "how 'bout we make a wager? Whichever one of us dies first has to carry the other one out of here. That seems fair, don't it?"

Doty's eyes narrow to slits and his face contorts into a grotesque mask as he roars with laughter at his own strange joke.

But nobody laughs with him. Tom Shannon continues to sit by the fire, staring at the rotating wagon wheel. The other men stand motionless and silent in the growing darkness. Oblivious to the riotous laughter, they are slowly turned by the setting sun into black pillars of rock.

Manly rises and starts away from the fire. "I believe I'll take a walk," he says.

"By all means," Doty calls after him, "take a stroll and explore our lovely little valley. Maybe you'd like to invest in a quarter section and build yourself a cabin overlooking the salt marsh."

Even after he has passed more than a hundred yards away, Manly can still hear Doty's laughter.

CHAPTER THREE

※

THE DREAMS OF EMIGRANTS

*Our manifest destiny is to overspread the continent allotted by Provi-
dence for the free development of our yearly multiplying millions.*
—JOHN LOUIS O'SULLIVAN,
United States Magazine and Democratic Review, 1845

Not far from Mesquite Flats, a nameless wash winds its way
down through the Funeral Mountains before breaking free
of its canyon walls and casting its alluvium out over the sandy
plains of north-central Death Valley.

If you bother to poke around the hard-packed, bone-dry soil
of this canyon, you might come across a rusted square nail or
weathered chunk of oak buried in the rubble or tangled in the
roots of a creosote bush. If you're fortunate enough to stumble

upon such a relic, it just could be part of a wagon or supply trunk or water barrel dating back a century or more.

Finding pioneer artifacts along old desert trails is trickier these days than it was a few decades ago. But it's still possible, mainly due to the sheer numbers of people who made the journey west in the mid-nineteenth century. In the year 1849 alone, more than forty thousand American argonauts traveled from East Coast to West in covered wagons. Along the way they left behind thousands of tons of clothing, supplies, weapons, and tools. Some broke up their wagons, packing the bare necessities and leaving the rest in a heap before heading off on foot to beat the coming snows in the Rockies or Sierras.

But material goods weren't the only valuables abandoned by pioneer families on their journey west. Thousands left their sons, daughters, brothers, sisters, parents, and fellow travelers in graves along the side of the trail or overlooking some rare restful spot. Their deaths can be traced to a variety of causes, including falls from wagons, blows to the head, drownings, pneumonia, chicken pox, arrow punctures, bullet and knife wounds, cholera, dysentery, influenza, starvation, dehydration, snake bite, measles, poisoned food, and poisoned water.

Back when my fifth-grade teacher, Mrs. Felix, taught our class about the trials this country's pioneers endured on their way west, I was struck with awe and respect for these stubborn, committed, and unbelievably fearless (if a bit foolish) nineteenth-century Americans. They became heroes for me right alongside Sandy Koufax, Elvis Presley, and the Lone Ranger. I also remember being surprised that our nation's Western trailblazers were not held in greater reverence by twentieth-century Americans. Sure, there were a few statues of pioneers plunked down in front of civic buildings here and there around Los Angeles, where I grew up in the 1950s and '60s. But for the most part the argonauts of the 1840s and '50s were little more than dusty museum mannequins and sepia-toned drawings in tour books. And I sense that today, our pioneer forefathers are thought of even less often.

Moreover, they are often misunderstood. We of the twenty-first century—maybe because we find it hard to visualize lifestyles other than our own—seem hopelessly bound to the theory that nineteenth-century Americans were drawn from one side of this country to the other by the allure of wealth, the gold-rush fever so often portrayed in Western novels, television shows, and movies. Yet all it takes is an hour or two of wandering around the harsh territory they crossed to understand there had to be more to this journey than mere greed and the temptation of material objects.

Stumble through the razor-sharp spires of the Devil's Golf Course or across the barren volcanic terrain around Ubehebe Crater, or along the salt-encrusted puddle called Badwater. Then ask yourself how much wealth you'd need to be promised; how far you'd be willing to travel in exchange for the unbelievably small chance of earning anything at all. Remember, we're talking travel in wagons or on foot, with no certainty of where you are and what lies beyond the next mirage.

Sure, there were those who hoped to strike it rich in the California goldfields; it was this initial rush that set thousands of others to *thinking* about such a journey. But the relatively small percentage of individuals who sought mineral riches from the earth do not account for the bulk of those who eventually made the journey from east to west. For every man who dreamed of digging holes in the ground, a dozen others yearned to run that same earth through their fingers; to turn it over and sow it with seed and watch the growth of wheat or corn or hay.

No, the proverbial pot of gold at the end of the rainbow did not motivate the majority of this country's westward-bound pioneers. It was something bigger; call it the pursuit of a new beginning, a new Plymouth landing, albeit in California, Oregon, or Washington this time. The westward movement was a chance—perhaps the first and last that most families would have—to leave the crowded East Coast behind, to obtain land, to build a home, to carve out a bright new future for their children. And it represented a man's best hope for preserving his family name with honor beyond his own lifetime.

In many respects, the move west was the natural outgrowth of an intellectual, emotional, and often spiritual vision; a vision leading tens of thousands to embark on a quest as meaningful as the Exodus or the Crusades; as mystical as the search for the Holy Grail. To establish a new life was as close as any of these mortal men and women would come to experiencing their own resurrection. And all were clearly willing to gamble their worldly belongings, their personal safety, their past achievements and future potential, to embark on such a holy journey.

Unfortunately, as inspirational as their motives may have been, the pioneers of the mid-1800s were in many cases foolish, stubborn, and unobservant, so keen was their desire to reach the far western shores of our nation. Although traveling generally westward was a reasonable goal, they should have been able to observe early on that all western mountain ranges ran north to south, and that by following any one of the natural valleys running alongside these ranges in a southerly direction, a party would eventually reach flatter terrain, from which westward travel would be easier. Even Lewis and Clark—though their route tracked essentially westward—learned to detour north and south throughout their journey to take advantage of the natural topographic features of the landscape.

But the men and women who entered Death Valley in December 1849 had stubbornly climbed mountains, descended into gorges, crossed searing salt flats, and basically ignored the natural passages open to them in the form of valleys and arroyos tracking south all along their route of travel. All so that they could continue west. All because they couldn't bear to travel south or north any longer than was absolutely necessary. The only wagon to escape Death Valley was that of the Wade family, who eventually left the others behind and headed south. Arriving safely in Southern California several weeks later, the Wades proved that even in this godforsaken valley of death, salvation could be found by simply abandoning the stubborn insistence that one must travel due west to reach the goal.

And yet, despite their stubbornness, it may be that salvation was nevertheless visited upon those who stayed behind, because the winter of 1849–50 still ranks as one of the mildest and wettest in the region's history. This is shown by the Bennett-Arcane party's own records of where they found water and in what quantities. William Lewis Manly's book *Death Valley in '49* talks of finding frozen water in the cracks of boulders in the Panamint Mountains and of crossing stretches of snow in those same mountains, snow that might not have been there had it been a more typical winter.

Other tales of pioneers in the late 1840s and early '50s tell of a similar stubborn insistence upon westward travel. In 1846, members of the Donner Party became trapped not in a saline trench but high in the Sierras, surrounded by deep winter snow, bitter cold temperatures, and dwindling food supplies. And though these two environments are almost diametrically opposed, both parties arrived at their fate by similarly following questionable maps that depicted "shortcuts."

Both tales have attained epic stature as models of bravery and resolute dedication to a cause, though the parties involved might just as easily be cited for recklessness, inflexibility, gullibility, and blind allegiance to a largely undefined cause. And yet in the end they did leave behind a heritage of greatness, of determination and faith. And yes, of stubbornness too, but the sort of steadfastness we Americans admire in people who won't accept the status quo, who are willing to take risks, who question authority and refuse to follow accepted rules if promising alternatives are available. It seems, in other words, that the pioneers of 1849 were just as surely rebels as they were God-fearing, law-abiding citizens; they were every bit as radical and innovative in some respects as they were staid and traditional in others. In short, they embodied that pigheaded American spirit that has defined our people for more than two centuries, while similarly reflecting the traditional values and beliefs of the democratic system.

And so we delight in finding traces of their passage upon the land. We like to imagine what their thoughts might have been when first encountering seemingly endless deserts, deep saline valleys, or a range of barren peaks that appeared impenetrable, yet had to be crossed. We are beguiled by the thought that traces of our American heritage might be found lying beneath the sand that has piled up for fifteen decades along the windward side of a granite boulder. Or resting alongside a slag of shale high atop a windswept mountain. Or lurking between the clapboard walls of a splintered shack in some deserted mining town. Or maybe even lying right out in the open under the hot sun on a stretch of desert dozens of miles and 150 years from the nearest twenty-first-century thoroughfare.

CHAPTER FOUR

EARTH, WATER, AND FIRE

I have heard complaint that the thermometer failed to show the true heat because the mercury dried up. Everything dries; wagons dry; men dry; chickens dry; there is no juice left in anything living or dead, by the close of summer.

—J. R. ROSS,
Mineral Resource Survey of Death Valley, 1868

Before there were sophisticated instruments to record and analyze ground and air temperatures of Death Valley, people already knew it was an uncommonly hot, dry place. That's why ancestors of the Shoshones called it *Tomesha*—Ground on Fire. It's why the first white men named it Death Valley. They knew; they sensed that this was a place of foreboding, a place where elements were at their most basic, sharp and clear and exposed to view.

The same is true of the valley's geology. References to its striking rock formations, narrow canyons, tilted layers of limestone, and undulating fields of sand are found in pioneer diaries and the later accounts of men who entered seeking gold and silver. They may not have known that this was one of the most geologically diverse of all the world's desert regions, but they recognized there was something extraordinary about the lay of the land.

Ancient peoples and white prospectors alike appreciated that the nature and effects of water here were simultaneously all-pervading and in absentia. The valley floor exhibited all the signs of having once been a virtual inland sea, yet its pools of water were decidedly undrinkable. There were springs that provided life-sustaining water in amounts so small it was measured in drips per hour. Yet there also were sources of fresh, clear water that poured forth in quantities that seemed far too great for this arid landscape.

Earth, water, and fire—three pivotal ingredients in this desert laboratory called Death Valley. Three dynamics working in concert to test those who come here. Three forces deciding together what will live and what will die here; who will survive and who will perish.

Upon entering and walking the ground of Death Valley, an observant visitor will quickly spot the diversity of ground surfaces. Some deserts are largely sand, others gravel, and still others volcanic in nature. But Death Valley's floor exhibits dozens of surface types within a fairly confined space. The same is true of the elevated portions of this landscape—the canyons and cliffs and mountain peaks. The wildly varied display of geologic shapes and forms and colors is nothing short of remarkable, offering examples from nearly all of the earth's geologic eras.

Among the most recognizable surfaces in Death Valley are the salt flats that dominate the valley floor. At Badwater, more than two hundred feet below sea level, you can stroll out into the sink and see that the snowy expanse before you is actually made of salt crystals, millions and millions of granules that look just like table salt.

Farther north you can pick your way across the sharp salt spires of the Devil's Golf Course. Salt crystals grow naturally on the moist saline floor of the valley, but periodic flooding usually smoothes their edges and causes the crystals to go back into solution. But the Devil's Golf Course lies above the level of most flooding that occurs on the valley floor. Any water that emerges from the underlying soil evaporates quickly in Death Valley's desert heat, leaving behind a salty deposit. In this fashion—not unlike stalagmites in a cave—the salt spires grow slowly, as little as one inch in three decades. And because there is no periodic flooding to wear away the edges of the salt, it grows into incredibly complex, sharp-edged pinnacles. Rain, wind, and blowing sand gradually carve the pinnacles into strange and eerie formations, sometimes rising as high as three feet above the ground. Walking across this jagged surface is a tricky business. If you fall, you'll get a nasty cut on your elbows or arms, made worse by the fact that this cut is immediately packed with stinging salt.

Another sort of ground surface—desert pavement—is common in the upper reaches of the valley floor, above the level of the salt pan and along the lower stretches of alluvial fans that descend from the mouths of mountain canyons. This surface is a hard-packed conglomeration of rounded pebbles that look a lot like an aggregate driveway or the kind of garden stepping stones made of packed gravel or river rock. Walking across desert pavement is a lot like walking on an exposed-aggregate driveway or path. The surface is solid, firm, and almost completely free of loose rocks to stumble over. It is one of the few desert surfaces that environmental groups believe can be hiked and even driven across without causing environmental damage.

Desert pavement is usually dark in color, stained by a coating of clay particles and bacteria called rock varnish. As common as it is throughout the Mojave, desert pavement remains a mystery. Three theories are offered for its formation: that the pavement is composed of rocks remaining after the wind has swept away all finer material; that the same effect occurs due to running water; or that complex processes resulting from periodic wetting and drying of the soil cause small stones to rise and remain above the soil level.

Even the geologically challenged cannot help but notice another major surface type in Death Valley, the alluvial fan. You can see them by the hundreds, spreading out along the bases of the major mountain ranges. When rain falls in the highlands above a desert floor, it carries dry soil away with it as it seeks lower elevations. Over decades of this activity, two things happen: a wineglass-shaped canyon forms, and the sediment being carried away is dropped as alluvium as the water leaves the canyon and spreads out into the lowlands. Over hundreds or thousands of years, a vast pile of material builds up below the mouth of the canyon. Its cone shape gives these formations their name—alluvial fans.

Seen from a distance, most alluvial fans appear as small aprons that look to be a hundred feet or so across. But as you come nearer, it becomes clear that these are major landforms, many of them miles from the base up to the canyon mouth. Mature fans can be many thousands of years old, but the centers of these fans generally feature a much newer wash, or arroyo, with walls several feet high. Over a period of many decades, flash floods sweep large volumes of materials through the canyons and cut ever deeper into these washes, sometimes carving them tens of yards deep.

Alluvial fans are nature's landfills, so you'll encounter a jumble of different materials as you walk or drive from the valley floor to canyon mouth. What you find is determined by the geologic makeup of the mountains above. Fans are frequently a mix of boulders, gravel, sand, silt, and clay. The largest materials are found near the mouth of canyons and the size of alluvium grows smaller as you move down the fan toward its base. Near the base, outside the main flood channels, desert pavement often forms where the alluvium is basically stable. An unusually large flow of water, however, can alter the shape of the main wash and flow over the pavement, cutting new channels.

When two canyons are found within a few miles of each other, two parallel alluvial fans will form. As they spread out, they will merge to form a third fan between them and then grow to become one massive fan with multiple canyon sources. Alluvial fans are magnets to hikers because they always indicate the presence of canyons above them. The larger the fan, the deeper and longer the canyon beyond.

Many people who have never visited Death Valley assume it is largely a sand desert, like Africa's Sahara. While it is not that type of desert at all, there *are* six major dune fields within the park. The largest is also the most visited and photographed—a seven- to eight-mile dune field just north of Stovepipe Wells. Two major dune fields are found in Eureka Valley in the northernmost part of the park. Two others are in Saline Valley and the sixth lies in the extreme southeast corner of the park.

Sand dunes are made of tiny bits of rock, chiefly quartz. Sand is formed over many thousands of years as the forces of water, wind, and ice decompose rocks to create these fine particles. Most of the world's sand was originally deposited along rivers and lakes or at the bottom of oceans. Climate changes over millions of years evaporated many lakes and rivers, while sea levels lowered and exposed other areas of sand to the wind. Wind, as might be suspected, is the primary natural force that creates dunes.

Sand dunes will form only in certain areas, because of three needed conditions. There must first be a good supply of loose sand in a particular location, such as a dry lake bed or the empty channel of an ancient river. Next, there needs to be a steady source of wind with enough strength to move these grains of sand. Finally, the lay of the land must be just right.

Typically, windblown sand will drop to the ground and collect wherever some barrier causes wind speeds to decrease. Cliffs and tall trees are such barriers. Other places where wind speeds can drop are hollows, valleys, and land at the base of a plateau. Most desert sand dune fields are found in valleys or basins.

Once sand dunes begin to form, they methodically spread out in the direction the wind is blowing until they have taken over a region of land. This movement occurs in two ways. First, the wind causes single grains of sand to move along the windy side of the dune until the wind speed lessens and particles of sand drop near the crest. As the sand blows, it drops and bounces along the dune surface; often grains are picked up again by the wind, repeating the process. Second, when a set amount of sand grains have gathered at the crest, some of the particles will cluster together and their weight will cause them to slide, or creep, down the steep back side of the dune, called a slip face. The sand travels down the slip face like a wave until it reaches the bottom and begins to pile up on new ground.

Sand dunes travel at different speeds and can become a problem if they move too fast. Some California dunes have crept forward as much as fifty feet each year, covering roads and threatening crops. Dunes can form in different shapes and rise to different heights, depending on the strength and direction of wind, as well as the size and weight of each grain of sand. The dunes on the floor of Death Valley rise to about two hundred feet, but the tallest of the Eureka Dunes are more than seven hundred feet high.

Like its sand dunes, Death Valley offers many other microgeologic features—small areas where unique geology is found. In a few canyons, notably Mosaic Canyon, marble walls show that limestone was once superheated to create slick, polished canyon narrows. The hills around Zabriskie Point are composed of one-time lake beds that formed, then were raised and twisted into convoluted badlands. Around Ubehebe and Little Hebe Craters, lava rocks are strewn about a volcanic

27

landscape quite unlike the rest of the place. Here, about two thousand years ago, lava moved through fault-weakened rock and, meeting water-soaked surface rocks, violently released energy in the form of steam, causing a barrage of rock fragments that blasted out at speeds nearing one hundred miles an hour. Liquid rock flew into the air, then tumbled back as hardened cinders, lava blocks, and volcanic bombs.

To walk through Death Valley is to travel through time and trod across ground surfaces as diverse in appearance as they are in color and texture; as varied in density, stability, and fundamental design as are the mountains, canyons, and arid flats around them.

On Sunday, August 15, 2004, at 7:45 p.m., Death Valley National Park superintendent J. T. Reynolds, having just completed the report he is slated to present at a Las Vegas meeting the following morning, steps outside into the muggy night to stretch his legs. As he stands at the edge of the parking lot, he watches an intense lightning show to the east, over the Funeral Mountains. A jeep rolls up to the headquarters building and park naturalist Charlie Callagan jumps out. He tells Reynolds what the superintendent already knows—that this is one whopper of a storm. He also informs his boss that he is heading up Highway 190 and into Furnace Creek Wash to see if any flooding has begun and to warn any tourists who might be in the area.

Two dozen miles east, Linda Small approaches the park's eastern boundary in her late-model Buick. The car is heavy, packed tightly with the belongings she needs to furnish an apartment she will call home when she starts her new job with Xanterra Corporation, operators of the Furnace Creek Ranch and Inn. Somewhere along the same stretch of road, Tabea Reith, age seventy-one, is behind the wheel of a Ford pickup, traveling with her forty-eight-year-old son Bernhard. Not far from them, near the turnoff to Dante's View, a white van is being driven by Matt Stokely, a Park Service maintenance worker.

Stokely has seen desert storms before and he pulls off the road as the increasing rain makes it difficult to see. Linda Small encounters his van and also pulls over. The Reiths continue through the pelting rain. By this time, Charlie Callagan has warned the drivers of a handful of cars to get out of the canyon. When he reaches the Zabriskie Point turnoff, he takes his own advice, turning around and heading back toward park headquarters. Meanwhile, Linda Small shouts to Matt Stokely in his white van and asks if she will be safe where she is parked. Stokely, who has already seen a stream of water coming down the road, tells her to get out of the canyon fast. He drives his van to a high point farther up the road. But it is too late for Linda Small. Before she can react, the river of water surges down-canyon and hits her car broadside, pushing the Buick some one hundred feet down the highway. Stokely watches from his vantage point above, certain that Small's car will shortly be engulfed by water. Farther up-canyon, this is exactly what happens to Tabea Reith's pickup. Swept up in the raging current of brown water, the car is turned over and over like a Matchbox toy.

As floodwaters head for the valley floor, they wash cars out of the Furnace Creek Inn parking lot and snatch two twenty-ton restroom buildings from the Zabriskie Point turnout, pushing them some two hundred yards down the highway. The torrent finally pours into the Badwater basin, narrowly missing a van driven by a visiting family from France.

Meanwhile, Linda Small huddles in pitch blackness as muddy water swirls around her car, which has wedged itself on a high spot of dirt and rock. The weight of her vehicle, filled with her belongings, is what saves her. As the water level drops, she finally realizes that she will not drown in her car. A knock comes at the passenger window and Matt Stokely is there, grinning broadly and helping her from the battered Buick. Throughout Furnace Creek Wash, and farther down in the valley itself, other fortunate souls sit in their vehicles, awaiting the light of dawn and happy to be alive.

When morning comes, a California Highway Patrol plane and helicopter fly over the canyon and spot the cars and trucks stranded in the mud. All told, fifteen people are airlifted to safety. Matt Stokely opts to get himself and Linda Small out of their dilemma without help. He knows the heat of the day is coming and doesn't want to wait around for assistance as temperatures climb. Little by little he clears rocks and mud away from his van as Small pilots the vehicle along slowly. Hours later they have made their way to safety.

The flood of Sunday, August 15, 2004, was the consequence of a mere third of an inch of rain. But it all fell in less than thirty minutes and was concentrated over a small section of the Funeral Mountains that drains via Furnace Creek Wash. That third of an inch also represented about 20 percent of the average yearly total precipitation for the region. The park was closed for ten days as mud and debris were cleared away, destroyed vehicles were removed, and the bodies of Tabea and Bernhard Reith were slowly extracted from their mud-filled shell of a truck. Thirty days later, a major downpour let loose farther south of Badwater, closing the south entrance to the national park.

In and around Death Valley, rainfall is extremely meager. When it does fall, it can be intense. Typically the pattern is for extremely long periods of drought to be broken by concentrated but short-lived downpours. Because the vegetation is sparse and the soil thin, very little rainfall is absorbed. Instead, water quickly flows from higher ground to lower, carrying particles of loosened mud with it. Badlands such as those found near Zabriskie Point are caused by tiny channels growing larger and deeper with each rainfall.

Perhaps the greatest paradox in this arid region is that it was all once a giant lake. Near the end of the last ice age, Lake Manly filled the present valley floor and was close to one hundred miles long and about six hundred feet deep. The marks of ancient shorelines are found on buttes in the southern part of the valley and clearly show the existence of this once vast body of water.

Another incongruity is the presence of a river on the floor of Death Valley. The Amargosa is the only major waterway flowing into Death Valley, and although its course today is largely underground, it was a full-fledged river during the last ice age, pouring into prehistoric Lake Manly after being filled along its way by a variety of tributaries, including the Mojave River.

From its beginnings north of Beatty, Nevada, the Amargosa River or a branch of it drains a portion of Timber Mountain, an ancient volcano whose falling ash formed several smaller peaks, some thirteen million years ago. Occasionally running above ground but more often dipping below, the river enters the Amargosa Desert south of Beatty, traveling southeast and flanking the east slopes of the Funeral Mountains. Intermittent stretches of shallow water allow the river to be followed as it passes south of Shoshone and all the way to the southernmost boundary of Death Valley National Park before turning north and entering the valley basin near Saratoga Springs. From here the Amargosa tracks north, both above and below ground at times, until it disappears for the last time in the center of the salt flats south of Badwater. Though most of the time it can't even be seen, the Amargosa runs more than 150 miles from its beginnings as a tiny rivulet north of Beatty to its eventual demise in the briny salt flats of Death Valley.

There is further irony to be found in the existence of permanent, even prolific, springs in this land that seems so parched. The springs at Furnace Creek, for example, are so abundant that the swimming pools at both the ranch resort and inn need no chemical treatments to keep them clean; they are simply drained at the end of each day and allowed to refill with fresh spring water each night. The springs also feed an irrigation system that keeps a grove of date palms thriving and waters the grass of the world's lowest golf course, at 214 feet below sea level.

When the Furnace Creek resort was first developed in the early 1900s, so much water was diverted that nearby marshes and wetlands began to shrink and dry up. Little of the original oasis is left today, but water conservation is now at least a part of the resort's operation guidelines.

Most of the largest springs in Death Valley are replenished by the vast aquifer that extends east into southern Nevada. The aquifer is thought to date back to the Pleistocene ice age, when rainfall in this region was plentiful and the underground reservoir was continually recharged. Today's arid climate means that virtually no water is being added to replace the water being removed.

Springs with lesser volumes of water are found all over Death Valley, usually along the upper reaches of alluvial fans or along the walls of narrow canyons. The springs that trickle down the walls of canyons are called seeps. The Indians of Death Valley knew where these water sources were. Today's seasoned hikers also know where they are, how much water they will provide, and how quickly a spring will fill a canteen. One hiker I used to tag along with believed in supplementing what nature provided, and he made a habit of saving old plastic jugs, which he would fill with water and stash all over the valley floor. He said he had a map of all his caches, though he never showed it to me.

Death Valley's reputation for record heat—the fire in its belly—is legendary, and many historical accounts make note of the extreme heat and its effects on people and animals. Oddly enough, the one place where accounts of extreme heat are absent is in the records of the '49ers who were trapped there for two months. The reason is that they crossed the salt flats during December, January, and February, when weather was perhaps the only factor that was *not* a detriment to travel.

But in subsequent accounts by miners, borax processors, and newspapermen, references to the heat are found in abundance. A good observer of life in Death Valley, and an enthusiastic recorder of stories about the place, John Spears included numerous heat-related anecdotes in his 1892 book, *Illustrated Sketches of Death Valley*. Many of them talked about life in

Death Valley—how everyday chores became all-consuming and how ordinary objects reacted in extraordinary ways after exposure to the relentless heat and low humidity.

A writing desk curled and split and fell to pieces. Tables warped into curious shapes. Chairs fell apart. Water barrels, incautiously left empty, lost their hoops in an hour. One end of a blanket that had been washed was found to have dried while the other end was manipulated in the tub. A handkerchief taken from the tub and held up to the sun, dried in a flash quicker than it would have done before a red-hot stove.

The Shoshones and their ancestors departed the graben floor each summer for higher ground. The earliest miners of precious metals and borax did likewise until competition, greed, and likely a sense of invulnerability led many to stay during the summer and attempt to deal with the heat. Some slept by day and worked the mines at night; they needed lanterns down there anyway, so what was the difference? Various contraptions were conceived over the years to produce shade, and a sort of water-wheel air fan was supposedly built and used by one or more parties living at Furnace Creek during the summer. The Lee brothers, when they owned Greenland Ranch, purportedly spent their nights in irrigation ditches, stones under their heads so they wouldn't drown while sleeping.

The effects of Death Valley heat on animals and men were noted by John Spears.

A thermometer hanging under the wide veranda on the north side of the Death Valley ranch has registered 137 degrees. It is in such weather as this that the sand storms in their deadly fury sweep through the valley, and even desert birds, caught away from the saving spring, fall down and die. It is a fact that since the ranch was established, one man has died from the heat while lying still in his house; and another, while riding with a canteen in his hand, on top of a load of borax bound down the valley, fell over and expired. "He was that parched, the head cracked open over the top," said a man who saw the body.

Depictions of the effects of extreme heat on humans—sometimes quite gruesome in their detail—seem to have been popular reading in the late 1800s and early 1900s, for there are plenty of passages found in much literature of that period. The influx of prospectors to the Death Valley region was so great that many newspapers probably felt obliged to run stories that included warnings to those who might be thinking of heading down to the valley floor to search for gold or silver. Other stories simply noted the disappearance of men in the desert, assuming the elements were to blame.

Beatty Bullfrog Miner, July 5, 1905

SUMMER PROSPECTING

During the past few days several very gruesome finds of dead and unknown men have been made on the desert in the neighborhood of Death Valley, where they perished from thirst. Prospectors, especially those who are unacquainted with the lay of the country, should hesitate before starting for there. Many were the emigrants who died from the same cause even in the winter time, and now with the hottest part of the year approaching, it is a hazardous undertaking even if one is familiar with the place where water can be had. It must be pleasant to be in the middle of some unknown desert with not enough water in a canteen to make it swash audible and a great number of miles of sand to be traversed in the glare of the burning sun before it can be refilled. The dead bodies of which four were found recently in a group with eight burros all dead bear out the pleasantry of the above, and a second warning is given to those intending going.

Also regularly appearing in desert newspapers were accounts of the stages of death by heat, again intended largely to frighten would-be prospectors from taking to the salt flats unprepared.

Beatty-Bullfrog Miner, July 28, 1906

PHASES OF DESERT THIRST

Half of the people dying from desert thirst perish in thirty-six hours, a quarter within forty-eight or fifty hours and all others of which the history is known within eighty hours.

The phenomena of desert thirst may be arranged in three stages, namely normal thirst, functional derangement, and structural degeneration. These three stages are made up of five phases—the clamorous [phase], cotton mouth phase, the shriveled tongue, the blood sweat, and the living death. There is hope in saving the lives of the victims whose thirst is diagnosed in the first three phases; but for the fourth and fifth death is certain.

In Bourke Lee's *Death Valley Men* (1932) he quotes a prospector who described suffering from the heat while walking through the valley in August with a friend, each of them carrying fifty pounds of lead samples they had extracted from a mine site and were taking back to their car.

Harry and me plugged along down that wash toward the car. Stumblen along, packen that ore through that heat an sun. Stoppen to rest an being drove on to walken to the car by the heat when we stopped. The first I noticed that either of us was slippen was when I happened to look at Harry's eyes. They was drawn way back in his head. His lips was swelled up. Harry saw me looken at him. I guess I was staren pretty hard. Harry, poor devil, tried to smile with those terrible swollen lips. Harry was tryen to smile an keep it up and it was horrible. I realized that Harry had just come in from the coast an was soft an not ready to make this trip. . . . I watched Harry go down the wash away from me. He was about a quarter of a mile away after he left me when I thought he began to stagger. I wasn't sure because I was looken through those dancen heat waves that were a-waven above the wash, an I was feelen pretty awful—starten to suffer pretty bad—an I thought maybe my eyes were playen me tricks. I watched Harry an pretty soon I saw that I wasn't being fooled. He got just like a very drunken man that couldn't keep his feet an he began to fall down in the rocks. I remember Harry staggeren around and fallen down an getten up an goen on again. An then things went blank for me. . . .

It's not all that hard to experience what the heat of a summer's day feels like in Death Valley. Simply preheat the oven in your kitchen to about 200 degrees and when that temperature has been reached, put your face close to the door and open it. The blast of hot air will be comparable to that experienced by stopping your air-conditioned car and opening the door in August at Badwater. The perception that the hot air is actually moving toward you, enveloping you, is the most common sensation of those who have ever felt temperatures over about 115 degrees. As your body adjusts, the initial shock of sudden heat will pass and there will be a pleasant feeling for a short time, a glow of good health and well being such as you might experience settling into a hot tub or sauna. But the body later senses that something is wrong and the early euphoria is replaced by sensations of fear and anxiety.

Curiously enough, heat stroke is not the most common form of exposure-related death experienced in Death Valley. Heat stroke is more common in regions of high humidity, where the body perspires in an attempt to cool itself but where the presence of so much water in the air does not allow perspiration to achieve its objective. In Death Valley, however, where the humidity comes close to zero in some locations at some times of the year, it is dehydration that leads to death, not heat stroke.

In his masterful 1986 book, *Death Valley and the Amargosa*, Richard Lingenfelter offers a compelling explanation of why people die from the heat in Death Valley.

On an average summer day in Death Valley, you can lose over 2 gallons of water just sitting in the shade; hiking in the sun, you can lose twice as much! Without enough to drink to replace it, the loss of 4 gallons of water is almost certainly fatal, and even the loss of 2 gallons could have fatal results.

The first sensations of thirst begin with the loss of a little over a quart of water. By the time you have lost a gallon you begin to feel tired and apathetic. Most of the water lost comes from your blood, and as it thickens, your circulation becomes poor, your heart strains, your muscles fatigue, and your head aches. With further loss of water you become dizzy and begin to stumble; your breathing is labored and your speech is indistinct. By the time you have lost 2 gallons of water your tongue is swollen, you can hardly keep your balance, your muscles spasm, and you are becoming delirious. You are likely to discard your hat, clothes, and shoes, which only hastens your dehydration and suffering. With a loss of more than 3 gallons of water you will collapse, your tongue and skin shriveled and numb, your eyes sunken, your vision dim, and your hearing almost gone. Bloody cracks will appear in your skin and you'll soon be dead.

An unpleasant but very concise picture. Heat in this place can kill. And given the size of the place, park rangers simply can't babysit all those who come here and decide to do something as irresponsible as head out into the salt flats in summer with insufficient water. National parks—Death Valley included—provide visitors with information centers, restaurants, hotels, gas stations, and gift shops—all the modern accoutrements that tend to make us feel secure, protected, and equipped with the things we need to safely enjoy our experience in the natural world.

But these places are not suburban malls or neighborhood greenbelts or theme parks. They are large tracts of land that have been set aside to preserve some of the earth's unique natural elements. Despite the conveniences, these are wilderness preserves where your life can be cut short in an instant by a tumble off a cliff, drowning in a flash flood, or dehydration on a salt flat just a few miles from your car.

Earth, water, and fire—all are natural elements encountered in many wilderness environments. But death is equally elemental, and it comes in forms as diverse and unexpected as the unsettling sights and sounds and experiences we have come to expect in a remarkable place like Death Valley.

CHAPTER FIVE

PUPFISH, PIPISTRELLES, AND PICKLEWEED

The true desert breeds its own kind, each in its particular habitat. The angle of the slope, the frontage of a hill, the structure of the soil determines the plant. . . . Most species have well-defined areas of growth, the best index the voiceless land can give the traveler of his whereabouts.

—Mary Austin,
The Land of Little Rain, 1903

When I arrived at Salt Creek for the first time, I saw a sluggish little stream dragging itself across a borax-encrusted flat—a stream whose banks were thick with clumps of pickleweed and salt grass, whose flow was unimpeded and completely natural in appearance. Most of all, I remember the solitude surrounding the little flow of saltwater, a silence allowing me to hear the hum of a horsefly twenty yards away or the flap of a crow's wings far upstream.

Back then, if you had patience and didn't mind the stains of salt brine on your clothes, you could lie on your belly with your head down at creek level and watch the comings and goings of *Cyprinodon salinus*, one of four species of the pupfish, which is one of two genera of the killifish, a species of saltwater minnow. The inch-long fish were there on chilly January mornings and in the sweltering heat of July, frolicking in the shallows and darting between pockets of shade created by overhanging bushes.

Because the tiny fish have no way to escape the high temperatures of their sun-heated creek, they have evolved over thousands of years to become among the most temperature tolerant of the world's known fishes. Testing the creek water with a thermometer one summer, I watched the mercury rise to nearly 100 degrees, and the fish were every bit as frisky as they had been that spring. Measurements by scientists who possess instruments far more sophisticated than my swimming pool thermometer have shown the pupfish to survive in water as hot as 112 degrees. Other Death Valley pupfish species, in fact, actually live in hot springs. And all have found ways to deal with the cold as well as the heat. In the occasional event of extremely frigid water temperatures, they protect themselves by burrowing into the mud of the streambed and slowing their heart rates to a state of dormancy, which lasts as long as extreme cold persists.

Aside from heat and cold, pupfish also must endure the high saline content of most Death Valley streams and pools—typically two to three times saltier than sea water. When Salt Creek and other streams on the valley floor evaporate in the summer to the point of near disappearance, the dissolved salts become even more concentrated. Tests have shown some species of pupfish to withstand this supersalty water to a level as concentrated as six times the salinity of the sea. They have adapted to these conditions by altering the way they get their water for nourishment. While freshwater fish absorb water through their bodies, pupfish have learned to drink the same water they swim in, excreting the excess salt through their kidneys and gills.

Salt Creek, a key habitat for *Cyprinodon salinus*, is just twelve miles up the highway from the Death Valley visitor center, then a mile more down a dirt road. But it never seemed to attract all that many visitors back in the days I frequented its banks. I remember one warm spring afternoon I spent wandering alongside the creek for hours without seeing another car, another human being. For long, unbroken periods of time, I watched the pupfish dart and glide and feed in the pools and rivulets along the course of the creek. Late in the day I climbed to the top of a nearby butte and gazed down on the twisting little watercourse as it traced its path across the marshy flats. The Salt Creek ecosystem might, perhaps, have impressed me less had it been removed from its larger environment—the lifeless salt flats and barren buttes that surrounded it—but taken for what it was and where it was, Salt Creek had a distinctly magic quality about it.

This is no elegy for a vanished waterway. Salt Creek flows on today, complete with pupfish, salt grass, pickleweed, and horseflies. There are, however, some newly added features, tourist-minded niceties like signs delineating the evolution of the killifish and the hydrogeologic history of the Amargosa aquifer. A half-mile boardwalk also was added some time after my first visit; the wood-planked, self-guided, sanitized-for-your-protection nature trail is punctuated here and there with garbage cans and tastefully worded placards warning visitors to stay on the elevated walkway and not to venture down along the damp banks of the sluggish stream itself or attempt to trek across the salt- and borax-encrusted surface of the surrounding landscape. Lastly, the road to Salt Creek has been improved and additional parking added.

Some may call me too quick to criticize; after all, nothing drastic has happened to change the overall appearance of the place. There are, I'm sure, even benefits to be had from these modest additions to the Salt Creek environment. The board-walk, for example, has made the site accessible to thousands of people who might otherwise never have seen it, people who may now be alerted to the fragility of the desert environment. Who knows, their voices may even have been influential in the 1994 passage of the California Desert Protection Act, legisla-tion that environmentalists believe has begun to slow deterio-ration of desert fish habitats. And so, increasing the number of tourist visits here may have been a good thing.

And yet it remains difficult for me to accept these addi-tions, these *improvements*, because the increased traffic in and about Salt Creek has created its own problems. In my early visits I didn't see portly tourists in rubber thongs and Hawaiian print shorts stomping down the boardwalk and cre-ating minor earth tremors that scatter the fish in all direc-tions. Nor were there bands of noisy children who these days race down the wood-planked roadway as if it's some sort of theme park queue. When they're not pushing members of their group into the creek as a joke, they're tossing Dolly Madison cupcake wrappers, used chewing gum, and rubberized action figures into the waters below. The stream is still there, the fish are still there, the vegetation and insect life are intact. But the solitude is gone. The quiet that was once as much a part of Salt Creek as the creek itself has been disturbed by the steady hum of the modern tourist (*Shortsightus bipedus*).

Fortunately there are other places to visit pupfish in sur-roundings that have changed little for a thousand years. Perhaps the most unusual pupfish habitat is Devil's Hole, a rectangular hole in the ground about nine feet wide, twenty feet long, and forty feet deep. At the bottom of this hole is the pool in which *Cyprinodon diabolis* can be found. Other subspecies can be found in the same general Ash Meadows area (about forty miles east of the Death Valley National Park boundary) that is dotted with isolated spring-fed pools vary-ing in size from as small and shallow as a bathtub to as large as a hundred feet across and twenty to thirty feet deep.

The Ash Meadows area, isolated and infrequently visited to this day, is the site of perhaps the greatest battle ever waged over an animal species, certainly over a species of fish. It all began back in the 1940s when Death Valley was a national monument, and biologists Robert Miller and Carl Hubbs suggested that Devil's Hole be made part of that monument, based upon the rare fish it contained. In those days, however, preservation of animal species was never regarded as a primary reason for creation of or addition to a federal park or monument. So Miller and Hubbs provided a geologic rationale—a travertine limestone formation in the hole—that granted them their wish. In 1952, President Truman issued a proclamation adding Devil's Hole to Death Valley National Monument. As a part of the monument, it could now be protected by a fence and locked gate, which was installed in 1956 to keep out vandals.

But other forces against nature eventually proved more powerful than vandals. In the 1960s the level of Devil's Hole water began to drop, a victim of nearby wells that had been dug to capture water for irrigation of grazing land. In addition, a game fish hatchery had been built nearby, tapping more water from below ground, not to mention introducing non-native fish to the area. As more developers, ranchers, and well diggers populated the area, the water in Devil's Hole began to decline significantly.

The depth of the pool in Devil's Hole has yet to be determined. It has long been known to be an entrance to a submerged cave system that runs for miles beneath the Ash Meadows area and likely beneath the saline floor of Death Valley as well. Unfortunately the Devil's Hole pupfish live and breed only in the water above a shallow shelf just three feet beneath the surface.

By the late 1960s it had come to the point that any further declines in water levels would likely expose the shelf and possibly cause extinction of the fish. A 1969 symposium on the problem led to the creation of the Desert Fishes Council. The group's environmentalists, state and federal agencies, and educators were soon joined by concerned members of the media, who began publicizing the existence of the ancient pupfish and their modern-day dilemma. By 1970, so extensive was the newspaper, magazine, and television coverage that the Department of the Interior was obliged to form a pupfish task force to look for ways to save the fish.

It was about this time in my late teenage years that I began to seriously reflect on the fact that there were other species out there besides my own. As an increasingly frequent visitor to the Death Valley region, I wrote a letter to Phil Pister, whose work as a biologist with the California Department of Fish and Wildlife was highly regarded. What I wanted to hear were the reasons—aside from possible scientific benefits—for preserving the tiny pupfish. I'll always remember one sentence of his answer to my letter—a response offered in the form of a question itself. "Must everything we do," he wrote, "have a man-related benefit, or does our position as the ostensibly superior species obligate us to preserve other species for their benefit alone?"

Pister's response served as my introduction to one of the basic tenets of the wildlife preservation movement—the notion that we, as the so-called superior species, should never decide to preserve another species or let it perish based on such factors as what their immediate value might be to *Homo sapiens* or whether they're in the way of any projects designed to advance human civilization.

Meanwhile, the other side in the pupfish battle began to organize and promote its support for continued agricultural development in the region. Tactics included the printing of bumper stickers by a Nevada county commissioner that read "Kill the Pupfish." Given the region's location on the border between California and Nevada, an intense rivalry developed between liberal California lawmakers and their more conservative counterparts from the Battle Born State. Most significant was the proposal by Senator Alan Cranston of California for creation of a Pupfish National Monument, an idea over-whelmingly rejected by the Nevada legislature.

Nevada news media strongly supported ranchers and farm-ers. The *Elko Daily Free Press* said it had the solution to the pupfish problem—an insecticide called rotenone, which had been used successfully elsewhere "to eradicate problem fish."

"An appropriate quantity of rotenone dumped into that desert sinkhole," read one editorial, "would effectively and abruptly halt the federal attempt at usurpation."

The war raged on for years, and what began as a local fight between conservationists and a few ranchers eventually went all the way to the Supreme Court, where—for the first time ever—a decision was made to set aside a piece of land to pro-tect a species.

Shortly after the Supreme Court decision, the closest land-owner to the protected acreage decided he couldn't profitably farm the land that remained, so he offered to sell his adjoin-ing property to the U.S. Fish and Wildlife Service. It might seem as though the battle to protect the pupfish was at last over, but a few unexpected twists and turns remained. With the landowner's offer pending, the local director of the Fish and Wildlife Service asked for input by an endangered spe-cies expert; astoundingly, both decided the agency did not need to buy the Ash Meadows property since land for pup-fish protection had already been obtained. But while it was true that the Supreme Court had set aside a small amount of acreage to protect the pupfish, it had also given the Fish and Wildlife Service permission and responsibility to buy addi-tional land and thus save all remaining pupfish in the region. Bewilderingly unaware of this, the agency declined to buy the property, and the farmer who owned it promptly sold his thirty acres—and with it all water rights—to a land developer.

After the mistake was realized, the Nature Conservancy hastily contacted the developer with offers to buy the land. But although the new owner was willing to talk, he continued buy-ing up more acreage and went ahead with plans for a residen-tial community with thousands of parcels. If such a subdivision was built, water use would increase to more than 300 percent of the actual water produced by all springs in the area.

At a point where it seemed nothing could be done to protect the Ash Meadows area, the Endangered Species Act passed Congress. Not long after, in May 1982, the Department of the Interior approved the listing of the Ash Meadows pupfish and one other species, the Ash Meadows speckled dace, as endangered. This emergency action now suggested that the planned residential development would be in violation of the Endangered Species Act.

During this period the Nature Conservancy had offered to purchase all the developer's land for $5.5 million and to manage the property until the Fish and Wildlife Service could obtain federal dollars to turn it into a wildlife refuge. As state and federal governments worked to pass legislation authorizing the money to do so, the landowner insisted on $6 million. Environmental groups began taking steps to file suit against the landowner.

When it seemed that an impossible stalemate had been reached, the National Wetlands Grant program of the Mellon Foundation loaned the Nature Conservancy $1 million and the Goodhill Foundation added $500,000. That gave the Nature Conservancy enough to purchase the land. In 1984, Ash Meadows National Wildlife Refuge was at last created; it had taken more than three decades after Devil's Hole was added to Death Valley National Monument for the remaining pupfish habitats to be protected.

The pupfish may be Death Valley's most celebrated wildlife resident, but there are a host of other species—bird, mammal, and reptile—in and around national park boundaries. Some are endangered, while others are doing just fine, thank you.

The park and adjacent desert support 51 native mammals, 307 species of birds, 36 reptiles, and 3 amphibians. Small mammals predominate, but some rather large ones can be found in the mountain ranges flanking the valley floor. Among these are bobcat, coyote, desert bighorn, mountain lion, and mule deer.

Birds are the most numerous species in the Death Valley region. In any given twenty-four-hour period, you have the chance to observe sandpipers, phalaropes, gulls and terns, pigeons and doves, cuckoos and roadrunners, owls, night-hawks, swifts, hummingbirds, woodpeckers, sapsuckers, fly-catchers, and crows.

You'll find them nesting in the palms and tamarisk at Furnace Creek, swooping through the upper regions of Funeral Mountain slot canyons, perched on the branches of massive cottonwoods in Cottonwood Canyon, circling the ruins of Chloride City, and wading in the Badwater shallows. Other species of birds are transitory, passing through Death Valley on their migratory journeys north or south—blue herons and trumpeter swans, coots and grebes, herons and cormorants, teals and shovelers. A flamingo was spotted one year.

Some of nature's most nimble and acrobatic creatures are found in Death Valley. But then, they need to be nimble to escape the ground heat. The Mojave fringe-toed lizard is here, living in the fine-grained Ibex Dunes of the extreme southeast corner of the park. This speedy little reptile employs uniquely evolved webbing, or fringes, on its toes to run across sand at speeds that have been clocked as fast as twenty-three miles per hour. It can run on all fours or—if it needs a sudden burst of speed—can rise up and run using only its back legs. The fringe-toed lizard also "swims" underneath soft sand when it needs to move to cooler temperatures. Scientists clocking this lizard have used small treadmills in the laboratory; in the field, they have been known to smooth out the ripples of sand dunes with leaf blowers at dusk, then measure fresh lizard tracks in the morning.

Clever tricks such as swimming under hot sand are the fringe-toed lizard's method for keeping cool. Other animals have similar techniques. The kangaroo rat, for example, hops wherever it goes, avoiding continuous contact with hot earth. It also can live its entire life without ever drinking a drop of liquid, thanks to its ability to metabolize all the moisture it needs from the fat and starch found in dry seeds. It conserves moisture by saving as much of it in its body as possible; the minuscule amount of urine it passes is four to five times more concentrated than human urine.

Death Valley's snakes, of which there are nineteen species, get most of the water they need from dining on small rodents such as our friend the kangaroo rat. The sidewinder makes its home near dune fields and comes out at night to create beautiful extended S-shaped trails that are visible in the morning if you are an early riser and there has been no overnight breeze. The undulating snake tracks are occasionally flanked by the footprints of tiny rodents, footprints that often disappear quite suddenly for clear and menacing reasons. Although this snake hunts at night to avoid the heat, its fluid movements evolved as an efficient way to climb the steep dunes and to reduce body contact with hot ground. It also sports hornlike protuberances above its eyes that act as sun visors to reduce glare if forced to come out in the bright light of midday.

Other poisonous snakes are found here, but the intense heat of the valley floor actually makes you safer here than in other parts of the Mojave Desert. Most of Death Valley's snakes are not only harmless, but are also hidden from sight most of their lives. The western blind snake, which is both blind and toothless, spends its days underground and out of the intense heat. It gets its moisture from eating ants and termites, along with their eggs, pupae, and larvae.

Other creatures in Death Valley survive by simply camping out in locales where water is permanent, such as springs, pools, and under the vegetation found beneath seeps from canyon walls. The extremely rare and reclusive Inyo Mountains salamander survives only in confined, moist habitats above five thousand feet in elevation. It spends its life under rocks where permanent springs or seeps keep the soil damp.

Infrequent desert wetlands teem with a diversity of creatures found nowhere else in the world. Five rare invertebrate species are found at Saratoga Springs—the Amargosa spring and tryonia snails, Saratoga Springs belostoma bug, Amargosa naucorid bug, and the Death Valley June beetle.

Many of Death Valley's least acceptable inhabitants—from a warm and fuzzy point of view—seem to thrive best in places once inhabited by man. In the mine shafts and tunnels, crumbling mill buildings, and corrugated miners' shacks of the Panamint, Funeral, and Grapevine ranges, a wide variety of less huggable wildlife can be found. Almost a dozen species of bats—from the small-footed myotis to the western big ear—make their homes among the rafters and beams and lofts of weathered ghost-town structures. On the ground beneath their roosting sites, amidst the splintered two-by-fours, rusty pulley wheels, and scattered rocks that escaped the pounding weights of the stamp mill, the Panamint rattlesnake often curls in wait for a passing shrew or pocket mouse or tourist.

Smaller but equally dangerous creatures also inhabit the ruins of buildings and mines—among them the Russell's recluse spider, whose bite can cause chills, fever, nausea, muscle pain, and flulike symptoms. In severe cases this can be followed by convulsions and damage to red blood cell walls that can lead to renal failure. Black widows, too, can be found in old mining buildings, but they are equally at home in campsite restrooms, under picnic tables, and in the dark corners of your motel room closet. The venom of the black widow spider, in case you wondered, is fifteen times as toxic as that of your average rattlesnake.

Perhaps the most feared spiders in Death Valley are tarantulas, but for no logical reason other than the fact that they are big—as much as five inches across. The males can sometimes be seen at dawn or dusk, especially in spring and fall when they stroll about in search of females. Otherwise they come out only at night and usually stay pretty close to their burrows. A typical tarantula's meal consists of insects, mice, lizards, and other small critters unfortunate enough to cross their paths. And though their size can cause heart palpitations in the brawniest of men, tarantulas are rarely aggressive and almost never bite humans. This is not to say their bite isn't painful, but their venom is no worse than that of hornets or wasps.

Worse-tempered but equally elusive are Death Valley's scorpions. Like tarantulas, scorpions are night-hunting arachnids that snack on spiders, centipedes, and other scorpions. The largest scorpions (up to four inches long) also feed on animals such as small lizards, snakes, and mice. The best way to avoid being stung by these nasty creatures is to always wear shoes, avoid walking through thick brushy areas, and never reach with your hands beneath a rock, ledge, or chunk of wood. The venom of scorpions affects the nervous system, and the bite is painful but seldom fatal. Across the border and farther south in Arizona lives a more treacherous variety, but Death Valley scorpions are more revolting than they are dangerous.

All around the Death Valley region, a host of creatures large and small spend their days and nights living their lives in this great, hot, arid sink. Some are charming and others repulsive. All are fascinating, whether they be red spotted toad, collared lizard, night lizard, great basin whiptail, rosy boa, coachwhip, patch-nosed snake, western pipistrelle, hoary bat, pallid bat, free-tailed bat, black-tailed jackrabbit, whitetail antelope squirrel, roundtail ground squirrel, pocket gopher, pocket mouse, cactus mouse, brush mouse, canyon mouse, piñon mouse, grasshopper mouse, house mouse, chisel-toothed kangaroo rat, woodrat, porcupine, coyote, kit fox, gray fox, ringtail, spotted skunk, mountain lion, bobcat, burro, mule deer, or bighorn sheep.

If Death Valley's animal population can be considered numerous and varied, the region's diversity of plant life is outright astonishing, especially given that this is a confined area with radical extremes in heat and salinity. Despite the severity of this stark environment, nearly a thousand species of plants can be found inside park boundaries, twenty-three of which grow nowhere but Death Valley.

The diversity of Death Valley's plant life is partly due to the region's location in a section of the Mojave Desert that represents a transition or overlap zone between the Great Basin (to the north) and Sonoran Desert (to the south). The local topography—ranging from nearly three hundred feet below sea level to more than eleven thousand feet above sea level—means a variety of vegetation representing three zones: scrub, desert woodland, and coniferous forest. The arid valley floor is further divided into subzones, or microhabitats.

In the hills and mountainsides above the valley, junipers, pines, and other familiar high-elevation plants and trees can be found. But as you descend to the valley floor, the severity of climate and scarcity of water make for some more interesting species. Plants and trees with a foothold on the valley floor have been coerced over the millennia to adapt to the extremes of this place through a variety of clever means.

The mesquite provides a good example. Clustering in thickets in nonsaline areas of the valley floor, especially near sand dunes, these hardy trees have adapted to the scarcity of water by trolling for hidden sources with roots that can descend forty to fifty feet deep—often as much as ten times the height of the tree itself.

Just as plentiful as the mesquite is the creosote bush. It's not much to look at, but this scraggly shrub is just as much a survivalist as the guy up in that unnamed canyon above the mesquite thicket. Creosote bushes survive quite simply because they don't let other plants grow. Botanists believe that the creosote gives off a toxic secretion that, in effect, poisons the soil to prevent other plants from growing too close. Only when a soaking rain dampens the soil below creosote will the seedlings of other plants temporarily take root. Probably linked to the toxin it exudes, the creosote boasts a distinct and, to most people, unpleasant odor. Some have compared it to the smell of fresh tar. The Mexican word for the bush is *hediondilla*, or little stinker.

Even more remarkable than its survivalist tendencies and foul fragrance is the creosote's longevity. Like the bristlecone pines atop Telescope Peak in the Panamints, some of the scraggly creosote bushes on Death Valley's floor may be thousands of years old. Botanists believe this is due to the way in which the plant puts forth new growth. When the oldest branches in the middle of a creosote plant begin to die, new growth emerges from around the edges. And while the original bush eventually passes on, its new growth—essentially a clone of the original—takes its place and forms a bush as large as the mother plant.

After this has happened thousands of times, small circles of creosote bushes—the new growth—begin to form around a central area of bare soil where the original plant once stood. In California's Lucerne Valley, an area of the Mojave Desert about one hundred miles south of the southernmost part of Death Valley, rings of creosote have been found that measure forty feet across. Using dating methods that include counting growth rings of existing bushes and performing radiocarbon dating of excavated wood chunks, botanists have determined that creosote grows about one-third of an inch per year and that the oldest and largest ring of creosote bushes (named King Clone by its discoverers) could be more than eleven thousand years old. Scientists think that after the retreat of the last ice age, the creosote was the first bush to take root in the Mojave Desert, and the plants we see today in the Mojave and Death Valley are clones of original bushes.

Survival in saline soil is critical to many plants in Death Valley. Species such as the pickleweed, saltbush, saltcedar, and greasewood can thrive in high concentrations of salt. Other salt-tolerant plants include the arrowweed, which gets its name from the arrow shafts that Shoshone Indians made from the stiff stalks of this plant. In one area of the park, just east of the Stovepipe Wells complex, the arrowweed have grown in clumps that resemble eerily stacked shocks of corn. On maps this area is called the Devil's Cornfield.

Salt-tolerant plants have proven useful to scientists looking for ways to genetically modify agricultural crops so they are more resistant to soils with high concentrations of salt. The key objective of this research is to isolate those genes that help plants adapt to high salt concentrations in water and soil.

When many people think "desert" they think cactus. Yet while the Mojave is rich with cacti and succulent species, cactus is in short supply in Death Valley proper due to extremes of heat, dryness, and soil salinity. Still, several varieties grow in elevations between several hundred and several thousand feet above sea level. Species most commonly seen include cottontop barrel, silver cholla, and beavertail. Dramatic in their scarcity here are Joshua trees—the signature plant of the Mojave Desert—which are found in only a few places, most noticeably at Lee Flat (west of Hunter Mountain) and southwest of Ubehebe Crater along the road to Hidden Valley and the Racetrack.

Many Death Valley plants have quite beautiful flowers, larger and more colorful than one might expect in a saline graben. Some of these are among the showiest flowers in the entire Mojave Desert. The large Panamint daisy is so flashy it was chosen as the logo for the California Native Plant Society. The delicate, lavender-colored desert mountain penstemon is found in canyons and washes, a soft contrast to the sharp-edged rocks around it. Other flowering plants that cling from sheer canyon walls but look like they belong in a lush greenhouse setting include the ragged-leafed rocklady and the Death Valley monkeyflower.

Some of the rarest plants in Death Valley are found in some of the most extreme habitats. Thriving atop the shifting sands of the Eureka Sand Dunes, highest dunes in California, is the beautiful Eureka Dunes evening primrose. This delicate, sweet-smelling species is found nowhere other than the sand dunes of Eureka Valley. Its large white flowers bloom only at night. Why? To take advantage of insect pollinators such as moths that never come out in the heat of the day. Growing on sand, of course, has its down side. If the wind picks up, the sands can shift, eventually covering whole plants. But if this happens to the evening primrose, roots sprout from the sides of the plant, rise above the sand, and form a new rosette of leaves.

Also found atop the Eureka Dunes is the shining locoweed, which is covered by clusters of silvery hairs that reflect sunlight and help the plant conserve moisture. Below the soil, the locoweed grows nodules on its roots that gather nitrogen from the air, an important nutrient not available in sand.

And then there are the wildflowers. The biggest surprise for many first-time visitors to Death Valley in the spring are the vast fields of poppies, coreopsis, and an array of other species laid out like a carpet that stretches to the horizon. The best time to see a spring floral display is in years when fall and winter rainfall has been several times the normal average. In general it takes evenly spaced rains over the winter months to coax out flowers in spring.

Many Death Valley plants have names as colorful as those given to the region's animals. Where else could you spend just a few days exploring the hills and gullies and canyon washes and find pickleweed and pineapple cactus, bitterroot and inkweed, spinystar and old man prickly pear, silver cholla and Mojave yucca, dead man's fingers and Panamint live-forever.

It was Edward Abbey who, perhaps as eloquently as anyone, noted in the mid-'70s that Death Valley seemed as hostile a desert as is imaginable, yet provided for a diversity of plants, though none in abundance.

At first glance, speeding by car through this valley that is not a valley, one might think there was scarcely any plant life at all. Between oases you will be impressed chiefly by the vast salt beds and the immense alluvial fans of gravel that look as hostile to life as the fabled seas of the moon.

And yet there is life out there, life of a sparse but varied sort—salt grass and pickleweed on the flats, far-spaced clumps of creosote, saltbrush, desert holly, brittlebush, and prickly poppy on the fans. Not much of anything, but a little of each.

CHAPTER SIX

OUT OF THE FRYING PAN

Hell, you think this is hot? Just wait'l August.

—Maintenance worker,
Furnace Creek, June 1973

In late June many years ago, I decided to spend a weekend alone in Death Valley to experience the summer heat. Not that I'd never been hot before. I had sweltered under 113-degree heat at the Salton Sea, hiked through a canyon at 109 degrees in Palm Springs, sat around a pool when it was 106 in Vegas, even endured a few days of 103 or 104 in Los Angeles back when I was a kid.

As I packed my supplies in the rear of my Land Cruiser, I thought back to a midafternoon recess on a hot spring day when I was a third grader at Loyola Village Elementary

School. I could still picture all the other kids gathered in the shade of the huge wooden overhang by the school cafeteria, playing caroms and board games and dipping flat wooden spoons into little cups of orange sherbet and vanilla ice cream. Where was I? Out on the steaming blacktop playground, shirt off and draped around my head like an Arab as I embarked on a secret desert expedition for Eisenhower. Even back then, I must have felt some affinity with the heat and solitude.

It was late Friday night before I could get off work. As usual, I was completely exhausted after punching dough, stirring sauce, and standing in front of a pizza oven all day. My feet were sore, my arms and shoulders ached, and my skin reeked of oil and garlic. Tempering my exhaustion, however, was a sense of freedom and joy. Behind me lay a steaming kitchen; ahead of me, adventure.

Not only did I have three days off from work, but a promising forecast of high pressure and ample sunshine cheered me as I tooled down the freeway. Climbing above the lights of San Bernardino, I at last left the brown L.A. haze behind and headed north on the nearly deserted road into the desert. Traveling Highway 395 through the Mojave at night is a surreal experience—an empty highway with a fringe of sage on either side and the occasional arms of a Joshua tree reaching into your headlights as you speed by. Into the early hours of the morning I headed north until a tinge of pink in the east greeted me as I turned onto State Highway 178 just beyond the old desert mining town of Randsburg.

This lightly traveled two-lane road is unique in that the pavement turns red at this point and stays that way for a few miles. I've never been quite sure why, but I've always thought it was appropriate—a sort of warning to drivers that hot and desolate country lies ahead. Red road at morning—drivers take warning!

By the time the sun was rising, I had reached Panamint Valley and the turnoff to Indian Ranch, where I bought a ten-pound block of ice and plunked it down in my cooler. Alongside it I set two six-packs of cheap beer and some plastic-wrapped lunch meat and cheese. Then I got back in the rig and continued north, climbing out of Panamint Valley and over Wildrose Summit, then finally descending into the summertime inferno of Death Valley. Actually, it wasn't yet an inferno because it was still morning. But signs were there of things to come; at Stovepipe Wells around 10 a.m., the thermometer read a cheery 107. Still, the dryness of the air can fool the novice; it didn't feel a degree over 104.

I had chosen Badwater for the site of my experiment; at 278 feet below sea level it's close to the bottom of Death Valley. Everything acrid, caustic, bitter, or unpalatable eventually arrives here. Why shouldn't *I*? My plan was to set up camp that evening, just after sunset when the day's cooling had begun and I wouldn't be as visible to patrolling rangers. Badwater, after all, is a day-use-only area. To kill time in the heat of the day, I wandered around the largely deserted grounds of Furnace Creek Ranch, taking an occasional dip in the ponds above the ranch, watching the mercury rise in the thermometer outside the back door to the restaurant and visiting with park employees—the few I could find out and about.

These year-round employees have a time-tested method for beating the heat; they stay indoors. Effective, if not especially imaginative. One of them shared a beer with me and told me a joke I only half remember—something about a prospector who murders his partner for stealing his two-by-four with the hole in it. By late afternoon I was filling my cooler again with ice and another six-pack of generic beer. Then I headed south for Badwater.

In later years I would realize that, in planning this undertaking, I had managed to do almost all the stupid things people aren't supposed to do in the heat of the day in the desert. Chief among these was not telling anyone exactly where I was going. At the very least I could have provided park rangers with a list of my next of kin. Then again, I wasn't supposed to be camping at Badwater in the first place.

Two equally foolish individuals were Charles and Randall Ludlow, ages twenty and seven, who learned their lessons about desert heat on August 2, 1953. That was the day they ventured fourteen miles down the highway from Furnace Creek Ranch to Natural Bridge Canyon, where the brothers planned to find rock samples for Charles's collection. The only official who remained in the valley during the summer back then was ranger Matt Ryan. If the Ludlows had thought to pay him a visit before their outing, he first would have told them it was illegal to take rocks from a national monument. Then he might have mentioned that Natural Bridge Canyon was filled with loose sand and gravel that would likely bog down their passenger car. And he probably would have relayed the fact that ground temperatures in August can reach more than 180 degrees. Not to mention that heat exhaustion can claim its victims in less than an hour. Most likely of all, he would have advised them not to leave Furnace Creek Ranch. Period.

Unfortunately the Ludlow brothers never went to see Matt, so they never had this enlightening conversation. Instead, they drove south on the main highway for about fifteen minutes, then bounced as far as they could up into the canyon before the wheels of their car dug deep into the sand. At this point they might have solved their problem by placing rocks under the drive wheels for traction. Or they could have waited until after dark to go for help. But these were two boys accustomed to the palm-lined beaches and soda shops and suburban neighborhoods of San Diego, a friendlier place blessed with mild summer temperatures and soft ocean breezes. They knew nothing about being alone in unpopulated desert regions or how to deal with a car buried up to its axles in sand or how the body's heat regulating system shuts down when the blood reaches 120 degrees. And so, blissfully unaware, they hiked out of the canyon and began to walk the fourteen miles back to Furnace Creek.

Two days later, a team of U.S. Army personnel was cruising down Highway 178 in a vehicle they had come to test in the extreme heat. Arriving at a point a few miles north of the turnoff to Natural Bridge Canyon, they encountered the body of Charles Ludlow, face down beside the road and hemorrhaging in the hot gravel. Seven-year-old Randall was found about fifty yards behind, in a position that suggested he had been crawling to reach his big brother. Neither wore a shirt or hat and their skin resembled that of a Thanksgiving turkey ready to come out of the oven. By Randall's side was a partly filled jug of lemonade.

Undeterred by the fate of the Ludlows and others, I felt no guilt or anxiety or fear for my life as I headed down the highway toward Badwater. After all, I knew what I was doing. I had no plans to leave the Badwater turnout (just off the main highway), I was carrying ample supplies of water, and I hadn't come to collect rock samples. No, I was here specifically to endure the heat, and my experience would hardly be the same if a band of would-be rescuers was standing ready to embark on a search mission.

I approached the whole thing as a scientific experiment. My plan was to set up a base camp where I could chart the precise hourly temperature curve throughout the day with the help of a large, easy-to-read Kmart thermometer. I also had lofty plans to record all of my actions and thoughts so I might later determine whether my thought processes had been affected by the heat. Finally, I planned to gather complex scientific data such as the length of time it takes to fry an egg on the hood of a car and the precise amount of heat necessary to explode a full can of beer. Somewhere in all this, I knew there lurked a potential research paper.

And so, with a tank full of gas, a cooler full of beer, several gallons of water, a reasonably good head on my shoulders, and a floppy hat to keep the sun off my face, I headed down the road, arriving at ground zero around dusk. The first thing I did was to pull out the thermometer and set it down in the shade of my Land Cruiser, where it promptly shot up to 119, just six degrees short of the maximum. Not very swift thinking,

I scolded myself. I should have sprung for another two dollars and bought the deluxe model, which registered temps up to 140. Now if it climbed above 125 my whole elaborate record-keeping scheme would fizzle. Of course the odds of it getting that hot in June were unlikely. The real heat spell wouldn't come until July or August.

⚓

By 8 p.m. it was still 113 degrees. Shadows had crawled down the east slopes of the Panamints and were now dragging themselves across the salt flats. Leaning against my rig and chewing on some beef jerky, I watched the waves of heat dance a final jig before nightfall. To the north, south, and west of me, the soggy surface of salt and ooze spread out like a wall-to-wall carpet of brine. At my feet was the saline pond that gave this place its name.

A remnant of prehistoric Lake Manly, Badwater today is nothing but a puddle. Though not deadly poisonous, as some early accounts claimed, its waters do contain high concentrations of chloride, sodium, and sulfate, not the sort of stuff you'd want to bottle and sell. The sole occupants of the spring-fed pool are a species of soft-shelled snail, a few varieties of beetle, and several larval regiments of the soldier fly.

As the sun set over the Panamints, I could see the reflection of Telescope Peak in the surface of the water. The water is more than two hundred feet below sea level. The mountain is two miles high. Where else in the world could I possibly experience such extremes? Such contrasts. Such highs and lows. In the light that was left, I saw the two trails that led away from the far side of Badwater. Both meander more or less west across the salt flats, one a bit farther south than the other. Why two trails, not one or three?

By 11 p.m. the temperature had dropped to 105 degrees. I'd been sleeping on and off in my underwear atop my sleeping bag in the back of the Land Cruiser with the tailgate up. I slept inside my rig instead of on the ground because the maintenance guy at the motel told me ground temperatures here are as much as 50 percent higher than temperatures just a few feet off the surface. Each time I drifted off to sleep, my mind worked overtime, thinking about all the descriptions of Death Valley heat I'd read. When I finally gave up trying to doze off, I pulled out my flashlight and looked for some passages in my copy of the 1892 book *Illustrated Sketches of Death Valley* by John Spears.

Imagine what the condition of the air must be, when having been drained of its moisture by ranges near the sea, it sweeps inland over the wide and undulating desert east of the Sierras, where the sun's rays beat down relentlessly from above, and are reflected back up from yellow mesas and white-hot salt beds. It becomes so hot that it strikes the face like a blast from a furnace. . . . Meat killed at night and cooked at 6 in the morning spoils at 9. Cut thin, dipped in hot brine and hung in the sun, it is cured in an hour. Flour breeds worms in less than a week. Eggs are roasted in the sand.

At midnight I again checked the temp—104 degrees. It was harder to sleep here than I had expected. Stronger than any other sensation was my unquenchable thirst. Nearly every hour I awoke with a sore throat and dry, cracked lips. I turned again to Spears.

A man can not go an hour without water without becoming insane. Several of our men went insane. One of them was a Chinaman, who had wandered away as soon as he had lost his senses. We hunted for him awhile and were then forced to give him up as lost. A few days afterward we went to a town sixty or seventy miles from there to get some provisions, when an Indian came into town leading our lost Chinaman, still insane and performing all sorts of strange tricks, to the infinite delight of the Indian, who thought he had found a prize clown and regarded it as the best joke of the season.

Some picture. A crazy Chinaman and a laughing Paiute.

Finally catching a half-dozen hours of sleep, I awoke around nine, with the 108-degree sun beating down on me. I decided to make some toast for breakfast. How? By setting two slices of bread on the top of my cooler. In five minutes they were crispy.

                        ×✦×✦×✦✦

By 10 a.m. it was an invigorating 111 degrees. Deciding on a short walk, I took the southernmost path away from Badwater, wandering across the salt flats 'til the trail petered out. The surface on either side of the trail was mucky, slippery as new snow.

Most of Death Valley's floor is like this—a thin layer of powdery salt with a syrupy saline solution just below the surface. You can feel it as you walk, like treading across a rubbery tarp stretched taut over a swimming pool. Here and there, the water breaks to the surface, revealing a beautiful pool of blue-green saltwater. The depth of these pools is unknown; scientists estimate the beds of salt and water pockets could be a thousand feet deep. If you stand still for a while atop this geologic bowl of brine, you'll hear its surface talking to you like breakfast cereal—snap, crackle, pop—as it expands with the heat.

The water in most Death Valley pools is part of an underground aquifer system extending well beyond the government-drawn boundaries of the national park. Another spot where it breaks to the surface is at Devil's Hole in Ash Meadows. Off-limits to all without express permission from the Park Service, the small, pitlike cave entrance leads to a vast underground cavern of warm water. This watery pit has been surmised to eventually connect with the pools on the valley's floor; the prolific springs at Furnace Creek may possibly be its outlet.

Although the depth of Devil's Hole has never been determined, it is known that the deeper you drop, the higher the water temperature rises. Apparently unimpressed by these facts, four men from Las Vegas entered the area in June 1965, changed into scuba gear, and set out to explore the mysteries of Devil's Hole. Two returned to the surface but their two companions—Paul Giancontieri, age nineteen, and David Rose, twenty—were never found. A rescue attempt by divers from the Brooks Institute in Santa Barbara yielded nothing. It may never be known whether Rose and Giancontieri succumbed to the heat, became disoriented in some steaming, murky passageway, or just ran out of air before they could find their way out of the watery maze.

Four years later, a thirty-five-year-old Czechoslovakian named Jindrech Vollbracht also entered Devil's Hole, which by this time had been enclosed with a seven-foot cyclone fence and three strands of barbed wire—in any language, a strong warning to keep out. But Vollbracht scaled the fence and dove in anyway, just ahead of his three friends, who arrived a short time later to see bubbles below the surface and to discover Vollbracht floating face down. At least they got his body back.

Back from my walk, I glanced at the time—11:30 a.m.—and the temperature—118 degrees. It's an odd thing. Even though I had just taken a hike, I had not yet begun sweating; the air was just too dry. To beat the heat, all I had to do was run a wet washcloth over my face. Even warm water felt amazingly cool because of the immediate evaporation.

Humidity in Death Valley is ridiculously low, sometimes nearly impossible to measure. Even at 118 degrees it's hard to work up a sweat unless you really work at it. And that would be stupid.

By noon it was 119 degrees. Pulling out a lawn chair, I sat there in my shorts thinking about contrasts, extremes. For some reason I began to picture the polar tundra. (No, I wasn't hallucinating. At least, I don't think so.) But I couldn't help thinking about the tundra because it's a pretty complete opposite of a Death Valley salt flat. One is a place of extreme cold, the other of extreme heat. Yet both are considered deserts. Funny, a person who dies from the bitter cold in the polar regions will remain perfectly preserved when found years later. And the same is true of the human being who perishes in 130-degree heat. He'll be there years later, too, unless the coyotes haul him away.

More comparisons came to mind. How do we preserve our food? We dry it—dehydrate it. Or take the other extreme and freeze it. Cold and hot. The top and bottom of the world. North

Pole and Death Valley. Telescope Peak and Badwater. Men and women. Life and death. So different, yet all so closely linked.

It's easy to wax philosophical about the Death Valley landscape. It's also easy to see why anybody already inclined toward the mystical, the spiritual, the pursuit of enlightenment, might choose to look for it here. More than a few of the region's fatalities have been linked to such quests for inner illumination. In July 1971, a twenty-three-year-old man from Chicago arrived in the north part of the valley armed only with a Bible and a dictionary. Donald Blackwell's thirst for truth took him to Mesquite Spring, from which he attempted a soul-cleansing hike to the top of nearby Tin Mountain, an 8,900-foot peak. Clad in a white suit and street shoes, his sun-baked body was later discovered by a search helicopter half-way up the east slope of the mountain.

The Inyo County coroner's report included these words: "Under the circumstances that prevailed, the accident could not have been prevented unless Mr. Blackwell himself had wanted to prevent it."

Also mysteriously drawn to the valley was Tarras Yarema, forty-two, of Falls Church, Virginia, whose personal horoscope had indicated his death was at hand. This was on September 11, 1973, and Yarema couldn't have been in a better place to prove his horoscope right. After walking off into the salt flats west of Furnace Creek Ranch in the blistering afternoon heat, he failed to return and a search was begun. The following morning his body was spotted from the air and a ground crew headed for the site to remove it.

"Death due to heat exposure and believed to be a deliberate act," read the coroner's report, adding that "further evidence supports suicide."

Edward Abbey went to Death Valley a few times. I don't really think he liked it as much as the deserts of Utah and Arizona, but he was there in the mid-'60s and wrote about it in his collection of essays called *The Journey Home*:

> Like the dazzling air, the heat is at first intoxicating—one feels
> that grace and euphoria that come with just the right ration of

Old Grandad, with the perfect allowance of music. Sunlight is magic. Later will come . . . Yes, out of the car and standing hatless under the sun, you begin to feel the menace in this arid atmosphere, the malignancy within that silent hurricane of fire.

———————

It's a good phrase, *silent hurricane*. Because there are no trees out here, there are no leaves to rustle, no birds to perch in the branches and sing. Even when a stifling breeze blows across the salt flats, there is virtually no sound. Just the crackle of salt and the white noise of hot air.

By 1 p.m. the needle of my thermometer had frozen at 121 degrees. Popping open a beer, I began to wonder what old Dan Cronkhite was doing at that moment. I really should have contacted him at his Morongo Valley print shop to see if he wanted to join me that weekend. Then again, this would be kid's stuff to Dan. Especially after that time in '64 when he went with a buddy to explore the Chloride Cliff area. Pulling out my copy of his book, *Recollections of a Young Desert Rat*, I read what he had written about the two of them hiking back up the hill to their camp after exploring the ruins below all afternoon.

———————

The lungs labored and gasped for fresh air and after we had been exposed to the full wrath of the sun for a time, the jagged peaks around us became blurry in the shimmering waves. Each armed with a walking stick, we moved onward and upward. The massive hill, which we joyfully skied down that morning, now loomed before us like a Mount Everest devoid of snow. We plodded up the steep incline, slipped in the shale, blithered delirious thoughts of pretty girls frolicking around a tree-shaded swimming pool, wondered of man's fiendish lust for gold, and of our foolish determination in seeking adventure. The swirling dust enveloped our bodies and formed rivulets of mud in our sweat, with the oven-dry atmosphere extracting what moisture the dust did not claim.

Progress was exceedingly slow, and at one point Gary became sick to his stomach, and a muscle-gripping cramp seized the thigh of my right leg. We stopped to rest, not sitting down for fear we wouldn't rise again. A thousand feet beneath us lay the dormant ruins of the mine we had visited, and as our labored breathing subsided, not a sound was to be heard. With fixed gazes staring blankly at the haze-shrouded Valley before us, a gentle breeze—as if from Heaven—awakened us from our state of stupor. Feeling somewhat better we turned and clambered up the hill. Farther up the steep face we stopped again, this time for a sip of water from our canteens, but were disappointed to discover the expectant cool liquid to be nauseatingly warm. The sun glared off the glittering mica and our eyes narrowed to mere slits. We spat cotton and ran our sleeves across our brows, then stumbled on toward our camp.

Dan later estimated the air temperature that afternoon at about 130 degrees. No such luck for me. It was already two o'clock and only 122. Funny, I didn't recall hearing about a cooling trend.

You can't talk about Death Valley without using the word wilderness. And though a purist might insist that any place with restaurants, hotels, gas stations, and a network of paved roads disqualifies it from that status, I would argue that any place you can lie down and die within fifty feet of a major highway is surely a wilderness.

People do that in Death Valley—they die in foolish places. In embarrassing positions. Some lie down right on the blacktop, perhaps in a show of solidarity with their deceased automobiles or awaiting a ride that never comes. Others just wander off through the arrowweed, keys still in the ignition, car purring like a kitten.

By 3 p.m. that afternoon the temperature was still 122 degrees. About that time, I had just finished visiting with a couple on vacation who drove up in a late-model station wagon with Iowa plates. It was an unexpected sight, disruptive to my self-imposed solitude. From its air-conditioned innards emerged a balding, paunchy man and his equally rotund wife.

"So this is Badwater, huh?" he asked me.

"Bottom of the barrel," I said. "Last stop on the Saline Express."

He looked at me oddly, then turned to his wife. "Let's take the shot right here, so you'll get that mountain in the background. Hell, that's a pretty tall mother."

"Telescope Peak," I told him as I dipped a hand in the cooler and pulled out a warm beer. "11,049 feet."

"You don't say," said the man from Iowa. He thought a moment then asked, "What are you doing here, anyway?"

"Meditating," I told him. "Communing with nature."

"We've been here two days," said his wife. "I haven't *seen* any nature yet."

"It's hiding," I told her, "It'll be back this fall."

"I'm Fred Johnson," the man said, extending his hand to me. "This is Barbara. We like to be adventurous," he added with a grin.

"You picked the right place for that," I replied.

"Last December me and the wife went to Alaska. This summer it's the Mojave. Can't wait to see the faces on our neighbors when we show them our slides."

"They're not the adventurous sort?"

"Jack and Betty? Hell no! They like amusement parks, the beach, that kind of stuff. Barbara and me prefer to see America like the pioneers did."

"More power to you," I said.

"Let's go now, Fred, it's too damn hot," whined Barbara.

Concluding that she doubted my sanity and feared for her safety around a bearded fool in his underwear, I smiled and offered to take their snapshot. "That way," I told her, "you and Fred can both be in the picture."

Pleased with the offer, Fred grabbed Barbara and they stood by my tent with Badwater behind them and Telescope Peak looming in the distance.

"This is great," said Fred, jabbing his wife with his elbow. "We'll tell Jack and Betty that this was our tent; that we camped here in . . ." he glanced over to the thermometer ". . . in 122-degree heat. Shit, is it really that hot?"

They thanked me for the picture and piled in the wagon, waving as they made a U-turn and headed back to their air-conditioned motel room.

That's what I like about Americans. That pioneer spirit never dies.

At 4:30 it was still 122. My belly was full of warm water that sloshed when I moved. By this time I was sure I'd drunk three gallons of the stuff, but I still felt empty and figured maybe I should eat something. So much for that idea: When I went to fish some food out of the cooler, the water was hot and the pack of lunch meat had fallen into it. It looked as though it had been slow-boiling all day. I made a mental note to myself: "Next time bring dry ice." As for the cheese, it had fallen out of its plastic wrapping and broken into little mealy curds that now floated freely just above the bulging cans of beer.

"What this place needs is a Denny's!" I recall saying to myself. Shit, now I was starting to sound like Fred from Iowa.

By 6 p.m. the thermometer still read 122.

I tapped the plastic housing of the thermometer and the needle rose half a degree. Time to stretch out on the lounge chair and take a snooze.

When I next looked at the time, it was 8 p.m. and the temperature was back down to 119.

I slept a few hours and awoke to a hazy sky. Rare summertime clouds had moved in and the temp had dropped. "If this keeps up," I thought to myself, "I might actually have to put on some clothes."

Like the spiritual pilgrims and the Devil's Hole victims, dozens of other unfortunates have died in Death Valley in a great variety of ways. In November 1960, seventeen-year-old Richard Hill became lost in a snowstorm atop Telescope

Peak. They found his body the following May. Two more mountain explorers perished in 1966, the second one killed while searching for the body of the first. One man died wandering around in a canyon after his private airplane crashed north of Furnace Creek. Others have fallen down mine shafts, off cliffs, and over dry waterfalls. A Japanese citizen died when he lost control of his car, and an eighty-eight-year-old Norwegian died in his hotel room. Then there was the man from New York who pulled his car off Highway 190 and put a .44-caliber Magnum slug through his head.

If one were inclined to believe in self-fulfilling prophesies, it might be suggested that Death Valley is simply living up to its reputation, working hard to justify the name it was given back in 1849. But there's an obvious difference between those few original fatalities and the more than one hundred that occurred in the twentieth century. William Lewis Manly and his fellow pioneers arrived in Death Valley by accident; their chief goal was to get the hell out of the place. Modern travelers come to the valley willingly. Their objective is to drive across its salt flats, explore its canyons, make love on its sand dunes, scale its cliffs, crawl through its mine tunnels, steal rocks from its washes, get drunk in its bars. The farthest thing from their minds is the notion that they might get hurt; that there might actually be a reason for the valley's name. And so, each year, one or two more people discover that reason the hard way. As for those who come here purposely to end it all, it is somehow fitting that the essence of their lives should drain away at the lowest point in the western hemisphere.

Around nine o'clock it finally got dark, so I lit my lantern and set it in the back of the Land Cruiser. With the tailgate up and my cleverly built two-legged extension adding another three feet to the bed, the rig had served as my cook stove, kitchen table, and my bunk at night. Before bed I drank another beer and played some solitaire awhile. Then, as I got ready to turn in, I spotted a pair of yellow eyes staring at me from a few dozen yards away. As I held the lantern in front of me, the rest of the varmint became visible—coyote. At first it seemed strange to see one out on the flats in summer. Then again, I was out here myself, and I wasn't even a native.

"Looking for a handout?" I called to him, but my scraggly little camp visitor held his ground, neither advancing nor retreating. He knew I had food; probably smelled my lunchmeat boiling. Eager to please him, I pulled the bulging bag of bologna from the cooler and bit it open. A poof of hot air emerged and I took a whiff, fearing the worst. But the meat seemed okay, if maybe a tad well done. Still, I didn't want him getting sick from eating rancid pork guts, so I turned instead to the bag of bread in the back of the car. It was hard as Styrofoam but it wasn't moldy, so I flipped a few slices toward the coyote.

At first he ducked and stepped back a few feet. Then he slunk closer, nose to the ground, before snapping up one piece of bread and devouring it in a single gulp. After eating three in this fashion, he took the last slice and ran off into the darkness. I wonder: Was he taking it back to a den of pups or saving it for a midnight snack?

Midnight—should be under 100 degrees by then. If I happen to awake and my mangy friend has returned, we might just howl a few camp songs together.

A Perilous Journey

JANUARY 1, 1850. William Lewis Manly has returned to his party and led them back into the deep saline trench he had briefly explored. Just twenty people remain in the Bennett-Arcane party. With much regret they have departed a spring of fresh water and continued south over a rocky road of desert aggregate along the valley's western chain of mountains, now known as the Panamints. Their hope is that the green valleys of California lie on the other side of this barrier. After several hours of travel, they encounter the mouth of a rubble-strewn canyon leading up into the mountains, possibly all the way up to the summit of the range. In good spirits Manly starts up the wash to inspect this passage. But after an hour, he walks back out of the canyon.

"It's no good," he calls to them. "The route is impassable for wagons."

Making matters worse, he stumbles while making his final descent and his rifle flies in the air, landing with a hollow metallic snap atop a large rock. He has broken the stock.

The party stops here for a while. As they rest, John Rogers, a bearded, grizzly bear of a man, shuffles around the area and comes upon a mound of earth and rocks about four feet high.

Inside this mound is a small well that holds about a pail's worth of slimy black water. Around its mouth grows a wiry sort of grass that has twisted together and framed the opening in such a way that the sides have been kept from caving in. It appears the wind and drifting sand have created this formation, since there are no signs of human hands in its construction. The water smells bad—a lot like sulfur or someone with bilious fever. Even so, it satisfies the oxen and the party decides to camp here. By taking shifts throughout the night, they are able to retrieve about a pail's worth of the brackish water each hour, enough to quench the thirst of both humans and oxen.

After breakfast a meeting is held. Almost immediately the question of abandoning the wagons is brought up.

"How long can the oxen keep up their pace on this small amount of nourishment?" asks Jean Arcane. "In some respects, I think it wiser to put them out of their misery here and now. We can butcher them, dry a goodly supply of meat, and head out on foot. That's what the Jayhawkers did."

Heads nod at his statement. For a few moments it seems the decision to start walking might be the only remaining choice. Then Asabel Bennett rises and asks for everybody's attention. Bennett is slight of build and unassuming of voice. Nevertheless he commands their respect as the eldest among the gathered.

"I, too, have spent a great deal of time pondering this matter," he tells them. "But I believe we should contemplate things more carefully before abandoning our wagons."

The others listen intently as Bennett speaks.

"I wish to make a proposition," he says. "I propose we select our two youngest and strongest men, stock them with food, and send them ahead on foot to seek a settlement and fresh supplies. The rest of us will camp here at this spring and await their return. I feel certain it will take them no more than ten or twelve days for the trip. When they return we shall know all about the way ahead and how long it will take to travel. They can secure other sorts of food to make us feel better, and after the oxen have rested at the spring we all can leave here with wagons and animals intact. I feel this is the best and safest way to proceed."

There follows some enthusiastic discussion of this new plan. Despite the concerns expressed by Jean Arcane, no one voices any strong objections to Bennett's idea. Their only question is whether the weak spring will provide enough water to nourish those who stay behind.

"If we continue tapping the water and filling pots and pans," says Bennett, "I believe there shall be a plentiful supply."

Henry Wade, a sullen, distrustful man, puts down his whiskey bottle and steps forward with a sour look on his face.

"What man who drinks fresh water and samples the bread and meat of an outside settlement is going to leave those green pastures and return to this desert waste?" he asks.

"He has a valid point," says Bennett to the others. "You, for example, Mr. Wade, are the last person I'd send ahead for help. Once out of this valley, I have strong doubts you would return to rescue even your own family, let alone the rest of us. On the other hand," he continues, "we have with us a man who I am certain will come back. I also feel sure he will be able to push his way through where others might fail. As for me, I choose Manly, if he will but agree to go."

Manly's eyes scan the circle of folk around him. At last he nods, agreeing to go if the rest of the party wish it.

"But I must caution you all that ten days may not give me enough time to retrieve food and supplies and return to this camp. I may have a clash with Indians or run out of water before finding help. I could encounter any number of unforeseen hazards and even should I surmount all obstacles thrown in my way, I still have no way of knowing the distance I'll need to travel before reaching a settlement. Speaking frankly, I believe you should consider this plan carefully before adopting it lock, stock, and barrel."

"Nonsense," says Bennett. "I feel certain we are on the brink of civilization even as we speak."

"Then, let us proceed with the plan," says Arcane, "and let us also send John Rogers. He is Manly's friend and strong as an ox. And though he is a valuable asset to our company, I am willing to part with him now under these circumstances, Indians or no Indians. The two will make a fine team and prove to be our salvation, if I'm a good judge of character."

"If indeed," says Henry Wade with sarcasm. Wandering back to his wagon, he sits down in the shade with his bottle.

"I'll gladly go," says Rogers. "What's more, I'll come back and get you all out of here, no matter how long it takes."

Now, arrangements begin in earnest. Jean Arcane kills an ox and he and Bennett set to work drying and preparing the meat. Captain Culverwell sits down and begins to stitch some new rawhide moccasins for the two men. Sally Bennett, Abigail Arcane, and Mary Wade begin sewing some knapsacks.

By noon these preparations are complete. William Lewis Manly and John Rogers stand before the others, ready to begin their journey. So thin was the slain ox that the two knapsacks are able to hold the entire supply of dried meat. Each man also carries a tin cup and a small camp kettle in which the women have poured a quart of precious well water. Before Manly and Rogers leave, the women insist on adding some spoonfuls of rice and tea to their loads.

Manly protests loudly.

"Ladies," he tells them, "you're robbing the children. . . ."

"You'll take it from us and mind your tongue!" snaps Sally Bennett. "In case of sickness, even this little bit might save your lives."

Wary of carrying anything that can't be eaten, neither man wears a heavy coat. Manly carries a light blanket while Rogers wears a summer-weight jacket. Both men have cut the brims off their hats so they fit closer to their heads and make them less noticeable should they venture near an Indian village. Rogers carries a good double-barreled shotgun and Asabel Bennett insists Manly take his seven-shooter rifle, since Manly's has been broken. Close to his chest, each man carries a sheath knife.

Before the men depart, virtually all the money in camp is collected and given to them. Manly and Rogers protest, but at last they accept the funds. Now there follows a long period of advice giving; nearly everyone in camp has some suggestion to make. Most of this is long in detail but short in value, since those staying behind know nothing of the trail ahead. Asabel Bennett advises them to stop occasionally for rest and to stay out of the direct sun whenever possible. Jean Arcane warns them to be on the lookout for Indians. Culverwell, the old sailor, launches into a lengthy discourse on how to chart their course by observing distant landmarks and watching the stars. The Earhart brothers advise Manly and Rogers to carry pebbles in their mouths so they'll always have saliva to swallow. The two Alsatians— Nusbaumer and Hadapp—offer volumes of advice in German, wagging their fingers like old women as they speak.

After they have endured several minutes of well-meaning but questionable advice, Manly and Rogers are at last ready to depart.

"Wish us well, my friends!" says Manly. "With luck, John and I will be back in a few short weeks with a fine homecoming feast."

With that remark, William Lewis Manly and John Rogers begin their hike up the canyon. A short time later they pass out of sight, leaving the rest of the party in the silence and desolation of the meager campsite.

CHAPTER SEVEN

THE FEW, THE BRAVE, THE INSANE

Eccentricities of Genius . . .

—CHARLES DICKENS,
Pickwick Papers, 1836

Any writings about the American desert would be incomplete without some mention of those rarest of *Homo sapiens*, past and present, who have chosen to dwell within its harsh expanses—those who have been willing to give up most, if not all, of the niceties offered by civilized society in order to pursue their chosen path of solitude, escape, wealth, enlightenment, or uninhibited lunacy.

True desert dwellers, those who willingly live in these arid lands and accept the environment on its own terms, are nearly always individualists. Some might call them crackpots.

It doesn't take too much research to discover that the desert attracts eccentrics as surely as the tree-lined lanes of suburbia lure conformists. In the case of Death Valley, this general principle can be multiplied by a factor of fifty or a hundred. The characters who have inhabited the region over the past century are nothing short of legends today. At the time, however, they were regarded merely as recalcitrant loners.

Take Bellerin' Teck, who arrived at Furnace Creek in 1870 and promptly claimed it was his. Hearing no opposition, he settled near the abundant waters of the spring, grew barley and alfalfa, brought in quail to multiply in his fields, and called the whole operation My Ranch. He enjoyed his solitary existence for about two years until a Mormon named Jackson came upon the scene.

"I own it," Teck reputedly bellowed while pointing at the land around them.

"I own them," the Mormon supposedly replied, pointing at his oxen.

Teck next spewed a long list of cuss words, this being his nature, but eventually got around to admitting that Jackson did have a nice yoke of oxen. To which the Mormon acknowledged that Teck had a nice patch of soil. Before long the two had teamed up to till the soil of Greenland Ranch. But Bellerin' Teck was too much of a recluse to put up with a partner for very long. Though details remain unclear, the story has it that Jackson beat a hasty retreat one day, leaving his oxen behind and causing one expert on the region—the late Edwin Corle—to question whether this Jackson could really have been a Mormon.

"It is totally out of character," Corle concluded in 1941, "for one of the Latter Day Saints to give up so easily."

Jackson's departure left Teck with one ranch and two oxen, something that should have pleased any ordinary desert eccentric. But Teck had begun to tire of Death Valley. Perhaps it was the 130-degree heat or the lack of female companionship. Maybe he had run out of challenges and the land was now too tame for his tastes. In any event, he departed the scene a few years later, leaving it to be claimed by the next set of valley residents, the Lee brothers.

If anyone were to doubt the collective proclivities of these four brothers, one need only consider their given names— Leander, Philander, Meander, and Salamander. The rumor was that the Lees were all running from one sort of trouble or another. What better place to hide out than Death Valley? That the Lee brothers were all mad is pretty much a given among historians. The only question is *how* mad.

Beginning about 1875 the four brothers ran a cattle operation out of Furnace Creek. A fifth member of the Lee clan, Alexander, later came to the same region and ran a stage route from Owens Valley to the town of Darwin. The Lees were known for two primary genetic traits—anger and lasciviousness. As for the latter, though no census has been taken, it is known that an impressive number of half-breeds (as they were called in those non-PC days) inhabited the region for many years afterward, each possessing a unique and telltale name such as One-Sock Lee, Peanuts Lee, Flapjack Lee, and a few others that remain as unprintable now as they were back then.

The anger supposedly possessed by all the Lee brothers is perhaps best illustrated through the actions of a half-breed son of Philander, who worked as part of a borax wagon team in the late 1880s. The first inclination that Smith (the driver) and McChristian (his assistant) had as to the Lee boy's temperament came when the boy announced he had a sudden urge to kill somebody. Then he calmly added that Smith looked to be a promising candidate. Smith was sufficiently impressed by the threat to leap down from the rig and skip off through the desert back to Daggett. This left only McChristian, who must have doubted Lee's sincerity because the two drove on. After a while, however, Lee announced he had decided to kill McChristian but was in no hurry and would wait until after finishing his supper. Fortunately, McChristian was nobody's fool and at their camp that night (presumably just before dessert) he announced that he had to go check something in the wagon. In the end, it was his gun that fired first.

When Philander Lee heard that his beloved son had been killed, he rode to Daggett hell-bent for a confrontation, but he was eventually discouraged from carrying out his plan through a combination of whiskey and a noosed rope.

Their reputations notwithstanding, the Lee brothers did manage to prove that white men could survive and make a living in Death Valley. Two of the brothers, Leander and Philander, also were instrumental in developing the Mojave Desert borax industry. However, according to Corle in his 1941 book *Desert Country*, their accomplishments were far outweighed by their collective reputation as malcontents and ne'er-do-wells.

Leander was the most prolific in reproducing his own kind; Philander could out swear any man in the Amargosa desert; Meander never did anything; and Salamander never spoke. And lastly, when it was established there were four, the fifth one, Alexander, showed up. Professionally again, they manifested diverse talents. Leander became a watchman at the borax works, where he watched until the plant finally fell apart; Philander became a rancher at Resting Springs, where he rested while his Paiute wife ranched; Meander meandered out of the picture; Salamander became a cook on a Sacramento River boat but was fired for trying to roast a Chinese; and Alexander was a stagecoach driver, but reputedly made his passengers drive while he relaxed.

Next we come to Death Valley Scotty, whose reputation as a big talker was exceeded only by the size and extravagance of his famous home—or castle, as it eventually came to be called. This imposing monument to Scotty's lavish lifestyle survives today as a major tourist attraction and historic structure in Grapevine Canyon, northeast of Death Valley proper.

Born in the 1870s in Kentucky, Walter Scott moved west at an early age and before long had become a turn-of-the-century impresario in the tradition of Barnum and Bailey. His tours with Buffalo Bill Cody's Wild West Show in the 1890s no doubt provided the education he needed to pursue a showman's career that would last until his death in 1954. He was not, however, a circus or stage performer. Scotty's theater was Death Valley, and his audience consisted of anyone gullible enough to believe his stories of lost mines and phenomenal gold strikes.

Throughout the first three decades of the twentieth century, Scotty's claims to have discovered the gold mine of the century attracted the curiosity of the public, the envy of other miners, the greed of investors, and the skepticism of newspaper reporters. Most disturbing to even the greatest cynics was that Scotty's exorbitant lifestyle seemed to support his claims; this only intensified worldwide interest in the man. Scotty spent money as if it were washing down into his pockets each day from out of the mountains. He stayed at luxury hotels. He staged cross-country train trips. He financed costly mining expeditions. And he ultimately built a multimillion-dollar Spanish-style castle, then furnished it with antiques and art objects from around the world.

Scotty might well have been considered the William Randolph Hearst of the mining trade, except that there never really was a mine—not a moneymaking one at any rate. Ultimately it would be revealed that the source of Scotty's seemingly endless assets was Albert M. Johnson, a Chicago millionaire who had come west for his health only to meet up with Scotty and form a symbiotic relationship that would last for decades.

Among the more notable of Scotty's exploits was an expedition he arranged in 1909, purportedly to prove to a few investors and a handful of nosy reporters that he really did own a gold mine. The names and specific dates are less important than the events, which Scotty staged as carefully as the scenes of a suspense movie or the vignettes of contrived surprises that await tourists around each turn of a modern theme park ride.

From the start, the six participants in this expedition should have suspected something. The trip to the mine was scheduled in June, a bad month to be trekking across the desert on mules. They also should have questioned why the expedition began in Barstow, a hundred miles south of Death Valley, although the supposed mine was said to be in the extreme north of the valley. Had the reporters taken time to research the matter, they would have discovered that a railroad line from Los Angeles could have taken them within a day's journey of their supposed destination.

But greed and naiveté were working hand in hand and all six agreed to the trip, which pleased Scotty to no end. He wanted these greenhorns to experience the desert in summer, and around every turn he staged attractions for them to view, each of which had a solemn or frightening fact associated with it.

"This here's the canyon where I was ambushed by two varmints trying to find the location of my mine. . . . This is a spot known as Robber's Roost, for all the attacks that have happened over the years. . . . These here are the graves of two men who were murdered while searching for gold. . . ." According to a newspaper account of the trip, the graves looked surprisingly new to one reporter, who poked around after dark and discovered rocky ground just beneath the mounds of soil. The graves were fake, like everything else Scotty would show them.

The trip progressed north to the ruins of the old Eagle Borax Works, located in one of the hottest, most desolate parts of the valley. Here there was a plentiful spring but also large numbers of hungry mosquitoes and fat, inch-long Death Valley horseflies. At this camp, while the men were alternately quenching their thirst and batting at bugs, all the mules suddenly disappeared and nobody could see where they had gone. Not to worry, said Scotty, he would track them down and be back in a wink.

Seven days passed with nary a sign of Scotty, and the men by this time were growing weak and disgruntled. Two of them at last ventured across the salt flats after dark in search of help at Furnace Creek Ranch. As coincidence would have it, Scotty came back with the mules the following day. Surprised that two of his traveling companions had left the spring, he claimed to have tracked the animals all the way back to Barstow before tethering 'em up and bringing 'em back. An explanation later offered up was that Hungry Bill, a rather jovial Indian who lived in a well-watered canyon up in the Panamints, had given Scotty a hand in his little charade. It now seems likely that while his partners perspired and cursed and swatted horseflies, Scotty was up at Bill's place, swapping yarns while eating corn on the cob and drinking cool, fresh spring water. As for the mules, they too enjoyed the shade and hospitality of Hungry Bill's ranch. Bill, it seems, had rounded them up on the sly that first day at the springs.

Walter Scott's outrageous exploits culminated with the building of his Spanish-style estate in Grapevine Canyon, in the northeast corner of the present-day park. Though he always referred to the place as Death Valley Ranch, it was and will forever be known as Scotty's Castle. Today, where once only Scotty and his silent partner Albert Johnson trod about in their dusty work boots, tens of thousands of tourists a year remove their shoes or wear protective plastic coverings to tiptoe across the same imported carpets and tile and hardwood flooring. Overseeing the proceedings as always is the old showman himself, who was buried on a bluff high above the castle. Scotty called it Windy Point, perhaps the most straightforward thing he ever did.

✕✕✕✕✕

In a piece that Edward Abbey wrote about the desert for a *National Geographic* book, he recalled his conversation with a grizzled old prospector somewhere in the desert Southwest:

"Why, exactly, have you chosen to spend your entire life in the desert," Abbey asked the man, hoping for some deep, philosophical response. "Just why do you love this place so much?"

"That's easy," replied the prospector. "Because all them other so and so's don't."

But a handful of so-and-so's have. Men like Pete Aguereberry, who carved a road well beyond his mine in the Panamints to the edge of a breathtaking view just so folks passing by could see it. And Shorty Harris, and Val Nolan, and Jean Lemoigne, all of whom spent their lives scratching about Death Valley's barren soil for elusive minerals, and all of whom are now buried beneath that same hardscrabble ground.

Finally we come to a modern-day eccentric who dubbed himself Wheelbarrow Tex. Why? Because he carried all his earthly goods in a wheelbarrow. Tex was a common sight around Death Valley in 1966, the same year that an enterprising Frenchman, Jean Pierre Marquant, made headlines by hiking the length of the valley in mid-July. Sponsored by a soft drink company, Marquant completed his journey amidst a throng of newspaper reporters and photographers.

Understandably miffed that he was taking the same sorts of hikes on a regular basis with no fanfare, Tex decided to stage his own walk and drum up some media coverage for himself. Starting at the ghost town of Rhyolite, Tex pushed his load up the steep inclines of Daylight Pass, then staggered to hold his wheelbarrow back as he descended into the valley, heading for Stovepipe Wells, about thirty miles distance.

The remarkable thing about Tex's hike was that he accomplished the journey without a support party, changes of clothing, or regular meal breaks like those enjoyed by Marquant. Unfortunately, Tex was not well-versed in the art of self-promotion. When he reached his goal, all that awaited him outside the Stovepipe Wells general store were a couple of dogs lying in the shade of an automobile carcass. Inside, two or three old-timers sat in front of a fan playing checkers. They may have looked up briefly when he walked in. But there were no reporters, no photographers, no television cameras or welcome banners awaiting him. Tex was befuddled at this state of affairs but did manage to entertain the general store regulars for an hour or two.

And a good laugh is hard to find in Death Valley come July.

CHAPTER EIGHT

A NIGHT AT THE RACES

Some researchers thought that gravity was the culprit and that the rocks might be sliding downhill on a very, very shallow slope. However, this hypothesis was discarded when it was shown that the northern end of the playa is several centimeters higher than the southern end, so many rocks actually move uphill!

—U.S. GEOLOGICAL SURVEY, GEOLOGY FIELD TRIP,
Internet page, 2004

In the northwest corner of Death Valley National Park, more than thirty miles from the nearest paved road, lies a little hidden valley whose floor is dominated by a two-and-a-half-mile-long dry lake called the Racetrack. The bed of this lake is roughly oval, but this is not the source of its name. Rather, it's the odd behavior of the boulders on its surface that, at some point in the past, compelled someone to proclaim this the Belmont of the Mojave. The Indy 500 of rocks. A geologic Kentucky Derby.

Ranging from stones the size of your fist to boulders weighing several hundred pounds, the greatest number of them can be found near the lake's southeastern end. There, a rocky limestone outcropping rises high above the playa bed and is the source of the greatest number of rocks. Each time a heavy rain or unusually strong windstorm descends over the valley, another few pieces of this scrabbly ridge break off and clatter down to land on the surface of the dry lake.

Of course, a handful of rocks littering the surface of a dry lake are not by themselves an especially interesting sight. It's what happens to them after reaching the clay surface that's so fascinating. Hike across the playa bed and over to one of the larger rocks and you'll begin to see what's going on here. Somehow, after tumbling down the cliff face and landing on the lake bed, the rocks proceed to move across the clay under their own power—not rolling or bouncing, but sliding along like hockey pucks. In the process they leave clear marks of their movement behind them.

I first learned about this place in the 1960s and can't honestly remember if I read about it in some obscure text about the desert or was told about it by someone in the same reverent tones that boys employed back then to whisper about time-space vortexes near Randsburg, alien wreckage at Roswell, or homes in our very neighborhoods where teenage girls might be glimpsed in their underclothes if one were to negotiate a bramble-filled back alleyway after 10 p.m. on specific weekday evenings.

In any case, when I arrived in Death Valley for the first time in 1965, I recall asking a monument ranger how to get to this place. I'm not sure if it was my being thirteen at the time or the fact that my parents were driving a 1962 Chevy Impala that led this government employee to convince me it was too far away and could only be reached via extremely rough roads, and that I should consider concentrating on visiting the scenic overlooks along the paved highways.

It would be another six or seven years before I actually made the trip to the Racetrack via a rough but quite easily traveled road heading south from Ubehebe Crater. Not only was the road negotiable in passenger cars, but back then when you reached the Racetrack, you could actually drive right out onto the flat playa bed surface.

But you couldn't then, nor can you now, actually watch these boulders race across the playa; if you could, there would certainly be a glut of handicappers lining the lake bed, each with a wad of tickets in one hand and a mixed drink in the other. No, these rocks move slowly, mysteriously, and never when anyone's around. The phenomenon was first noted decades ago, but the inaccessibility of the area lent it some degree of protection from the crowds down at the visitor center. The road was too bumpy, the distance too far, and the reward at the end of the trip was for years considered less compelling than the beer on tap at the Stovepipe Wells bar.

And so, for a time, you could drive right up to the Racetrack—even out onto its flat surface—and be entirely alone for a day or two without ever seeing another car or human being. It was the increasing popularity of four-wheel-drive vehicles that began to bring more people to the area in the late '70s. Unfortunately the additional traffic meant more car tracks on the playa bed, more rocks lifted off the ground and placed elsewhere, more names sprayed on the cliff faces and carved into the playa bed. Finally in the early '80s, the Park Service decided to excavate a huge ditch around the entire lake bed, which effectively put a stop to any more cars squirreling around out on the playa. It was probably a good call by Park Service personnel; despite the ugly gash surrounding the Racetrack, it was undoubtedly the most practical way to protect the natural oddities found upon its surface.

At the time of my early visits there, most geologists were convinced that a combination of rain-slick mud and gale-force winds allowed these rocks to move, but no one had actually been able to prove it. Ironically, the very weather conditions thought to cause the movement are exactly the sort of conditions that preclude anyone from watching the boulders in action.

This logic didn't stop me from trying, however. One late winter weekend during the early '70s, I tried to sneak up on Mother Nature by camping out beside the lake bed on a blustery night when rain had been predicted. Alas, all I learned from this outing was that rain-soaked playa mud is slicker than shit and that tents, too, can move if propelled by gale-force winds.

My mistakes were abundant. To begin with, I was woefully underdressed, wearing jeans, flannel shirt, and tennis shoes, and carrying with me only a medium-size flashlight and a 35mm camera. (I adhered back in those days to the minimalist dictum that said something to the effect that you should bring with you no more than you need and no less than, well—than you need.) Much later, as I sat in the back of my wildly shuddering vehicle wiping water and mud from my body and clothes while the wind howled outside, it occurred to me that a rope, some lead weights, a much larger flashlight, a half-dozen friends, and a box of large beach towels might have come in handy that night. At least I'd remembered beer.

Apparently the earliest recorded sighting of the Racetrack rocks and their bizarre tracks was made in 1915 by Joseph Crook, a mining prospector from Fallon, Nevada. I like to think that he was destined to enjoy this rare honor due to his already distinct status as a prospector with a wife, and one who tagged along with him at that! On the way back to his camp one evening, Crook came across the lake bed and saw the rocks with tracks trailing behind them. The next morning he took his wife to see the tracks that suggested the rocks had moved. Most reports credit his wife with the clever idea of marking the location of one rock by pounding a stake into the ground next to it. A week or so later, the two came back and saw that the rock had indeed moved slightly. In these early years, with no sophisticated scientific methods for measuring such movement, similarly simple experiments were conducted by others who happened upon the secluded valley and saw the rocks littering the lake bed.

As these experiments were conducted over the years, researchers started coming up with scientific reasons why these rocks moved. In the 1940s and '50s, most researchers were convinced that whenever it rained, the lake bed got extremely slippery, which I can attest to myself. Because the valley in which the lake bed lies has always been known to experience very high winds, it seemed probable that these winds simply blew the rocks across the slippery lake bed. Unfortunately, whenever the area was windy and rainy, it was impossible for scientists to stay on their feet, let alone watch to see if the rocks were moving.

Other theories were suggested as well, one researcher even proposing that wind had nothing at all to do with the moving rocks. He thought that when the dry mud surface got wet, the whole lake bed began to swell, causing ripplelike humps to form. If a hump formed under a rock, he concluded, the rock would simply slide down the hump and leave its mark. Most scientists were less than keen about this idea.

Another observer suggested there might be some connection between Racetrack rock tracks and crop circles, in that different trails sometimes ran parallel to one another and their paths were duplicated, just as a person holding two pencils in one hand can draw twin paths on a piece of paper, complete with perfectly matching twists and turns and loops. Most people dismissed aliens as the cause, however.

Other theories suggested that this was one of those strange vortexes on earth where laws of gravity or magnetism or both went awry and natural objects moved most unnaturally.

As the years passed, more sophisticated devices were employed, and teams of researchers conducted a variety of tests. Because it was difficult to plan such tests when natural weather conditions were just right, they brought large vessels full of water and artificially wet down parts of the soil in an effort to create conditions where a rock might move. But by 1995, tests had shown that it would take a wind of five hundred miles an hour to make even small rocks move across a muddy lake bed. No wind that powerful has ever been recorded on earth, let alone at this particular spot.

Forced to live with these new revelations about required wind speeds, many researchers over the past decade have begun to revisit a theory advanced by researcher George Stanley in 1955. Stanley believed that whenever a winter storm dropped a lot of rain on the Racetrack and the weather turned extremely cold, a sheet of ice would begin to form on top of standing water. As ice froze around many of the rocks on the lake, they would become part of the ice sheet. Then high winds, if they came, would begin to push the sheet of ice across the standing water like a massive raft. And as the raft of ice moved across the flooded lake bed, the rocks would travel with the ice. As they moved along, the bottoms of these rocks would drag across the mud surface and create the tracks that would later be found, after the ice had melted and the water evaporated.

Supporting this theory was the fact that ice-carried erratics—large boulders transported by glaciers and deposited miles from their source after ice-age melting—had been discovered in various spots around the country. This surely attested to the power of moving ice. Nevertheless, the ice sheet theory seemed too fantastic because the sheet of ice on the Racetrack could never be more than several centimeters thick. The theory was also deemed overly complex; wind and slick mud seemed sufficient to explain the process.

Still, Stanley had argued, the power of thin, moving ice sheets on dry lake beds had already been observed. In 1952, telephone poles had been plucked out of the ground like matchsticks and knocked over by the force of a wind-blown sheet of ice on a Nevada lake. Also, he reminded his critics, there were many cases at the Racetrack where two tracks had followed exactly the same pattern of movement, even though they were located as much as a half mile apart. This, he insisted, could only happen if the two rocks had been caught in the same ice sheet.

Even with Stanley's excellent explanation, contemporary researchers have countered by observing that other rocks show completely different patterns of movement than rocks just a few yards away. If an ice sheet formed and simultaneously encased all the rocks on the lake bed before being moved by high winds, wouldn't every rock encased in that ice sheet show precisely the same routes of travel?

And so, a final answer as to why the rocks move has yet to be determined. The ultimate conclusion may turn out to be that their movement is a combination of wind, a wet, muddy surface, *and* ice sheets working together to create movement by the rocks, but not identical movement. Perhaps a single massive sheet of ice forms initially, but then breaks into several smaller sheets, which would explain why rocks follow a set pattern in one general area of the lake bed but a different pattern at another location. In the end, nothing is likely to be decided until someone can come up with a way to be there and watch as it happens.

I have personally determined (as have most credentialed scientists) that even if someone managed to plant himself next to a boulder in a hundred-mile-an-hour wind and point his camcorder downward, it could be a very long wait. For all anybody knows, the rocks may move only a few millimeters an hour; it's quite difficult to determine speed by just looking at the marks. The moving rocks of Death Valley's Racetrack remain an unsolved riddle, just another one of nature's practical jokes on the human race.

CHAPTER NINE

MINERS, MURDERERS, MUMMIES, AND MARTIANS

Death Valley is where the rivers run upside down.
—CHARLES MANSON, 1969

Halfway up a sharp-edged slope in the Funeral Mountains stands the black-timbered hulk of the Keane Wonder Mill. In its time, the Keane mining district was a thriving community; it was said a man could always find his fortune here. All that remain today are a half-dozen weathered shacks, a maze of winding foot trails, some steep-sided tailing piles and, most noticeably, the massive mill and tramway terminus. Anchored fast to the rocky ground and held together by giant bolts, the imposing structure clings to the cliff like some gargantuan buzzard surveying the vastness of the salt flats far below.

The Keane is one of several sites in and around Death Valley that speak of the bustling enterprises once existing here. Miners toiled to extract gold, silver, copper, tungsten, zinc, and other minerals in these places. Towns like Rhyolite and Skidoo were home to thousands of people who envisioned another St. Louis or Denver or Los Angeles rising from the desert floor, the product of riches beyond imagination.

But far too many of the riches were just that: the products of someone's imagination, of overly wishful thinking. In due course, all of Death Valley's towns and mining camps, however prosperous they may have been, would die along with the dreams of their once confident founders. And there were other dreams as well—dreams that never bankrolled towns or built mining camps or extracted a single ounce of gold or silver. These were the visions of wealth propelled into existence by the lore of wandering emigrants and the tales of miners passing whiskey bottles around countless campfires.

The Lost Gunsight, for example, was named after a chunk of metal that one of the Jayhawkers scraped off the wall of a canyon and pounded into the shape of a gun sight to replace the one that had broken off his rifle. The metal was assessed as high-grade silver after the men reached civilization. A few of the men returned to Death Valley a few years later, but as in most tales of lost mines, they were unable to find the location of the discovery.

Still more notorious was the lost Breyfogle mine. Its lore and legend make this one of the West's most celebrated lost fortunes, right up there with Arizona's Lost Dutchman. At a camp near Death Valley, prospector Charles Breyfogle awoke early one morning in 1864 to hear his partners screaming as they were attacked by Indians. Grabbing his boots and running off into the desert, Breyfogle escaped the massacre but soon became lost as he wandered aimlessly in a region some twenty-five or thirty miles east of Death Valley's southern tip. While trekking toward a green spot on the side of a hill in search of water, he stumbled upon some outcroppings of pure gold. Thirst was Breyfogle's primary concern, so he quickly wrapped a few nuggets in a bandanna and continued on his way. Weeks later in Austin, Nevada, the gold was assayed at $100,000 a ton, a phenomenal sum in the 1860s.

Breyfogle returned to Death Valley a short time later with several millionaires who were willing to invest in developing a mine. Although the landscape looked much the same mile after mile, he remembered a couple of details to help them with their search: He had found the gold on a hillside with reddish earth, and there was a large mesquite tree nearby. Unfortunately there proved to be many reddish hillsides and a lot of mesquite trees out there.

Breyfogle went on at least a dozen expeditions over the next several years, as did hundreds of other prospectors who had heard all the particulars of his tale. But the outcroppings where he had found the nuggets were never found again. As the years passed, so many people were looking for Breyfogle's gold that a new word was coined for prospectors in the Death Valley region: *Breyfoglers*.

Another tale of lost riches in Death Valley concerns a Utah-bound Mormon who cut across Death Valley in the 1850s and encouraged his balky mules up hills by lobbing rocks at them. When he reached Salt Lake City, he left his coat to be mended and the tailor retrieved the remaining rocks from the coat pocket, only to find they were nearly pure gold. The story concludes in the usual way—lots of searching but no locating the site where the Mormon found the gold.

Then there is the story of Crisanto Santavinas, a young man who was hired in the early 1880s to build a furnace in Lida, a small mining town north of Death Valley. En route to Lida, Cris and his companions stopped at a canyon spring somewhere in the Cottonwood range. As they rested and quenched their thirst, one man took the time to dip his pan into the sand and swirl it with spring water. In the pan he saw flecks of gold. Showing young Cris, the man told him to come back to this place when he was older and he would find rich gold farther up the canyon.

The years went by and Cris never returned. But when two men talked with him in 1904 and asked about gold in the mountains above Death Valley, Cris good-naturedly told them the story. A few days later, workers at a salt refining plant in Saline Valley saw two men heading into the mountains. A week later one man returned, saying that his partner had disappeared three days earlier. Forming a search party, the men at the refinery headed into the mountains and soon came upon the missing partner, dead of dehydration. In his pockets were gold nuggets valued at about ten thousand dollars. Not only had the man paid the ultimate price for his find, but the source of the nuggets was never found.

Nearly all stories of Death Valley gold and silver discoveries end the same way. The treasure seeker comes upon the riches quite by accident but is forced to leave and return for them later. When he returns he is unable to locate his find. In the end, the seeker leaves empty-handed. Or doesn't leave at all. There is delicious irony in these legends of lost riches. In each story, the earth—the keeper of the treasure—simultaneously tempts and threatens her violators; the mistress beguiles then betrays her suitors.

And as the treasures were lost and found, as the prospectors and their corporate backers went broke and sometimes perished in the desert, an uneasy aura began to descend over the landscape. A reputation was well in the making for this arid, sun-dried wasteland.

Today, more than a century and a half after the first white men set foot in Death Valley, its somber reputation and unsettling atmosphere are entrenched. Experimental Air Force jets now scream over the region at seven times the speed of sound, and tourists speed down the highway with the security of satellite directional systems, but in many ways it may as well be the late 1800s. That same brooding atmosphere continues to settle like drifting sand around the ruins of towns and shuttered mine shafts and deep inside the narrow passages of dim, secluded canyons. I have felt it whirl round me like a filmy specter while probing the narrow confines of Red Wall Canyon. I have heard the whisper of voices in Schwaub and Leadfield and Cerro Gordo. And it has passed right through me, cold as ice and wailing like a banshee, as I have huddled in makeshift winter camps in the Panamints or in the musty darkness of a miner's shack above the Echo Canyon road.

This is a place that hints of secrets, that tucks its beauty deep inside narrow canyons, buries its treasures beneath tons of earth, hoards its water beneath the soil. And continues to attract a never-ending stream of humans intent upon wresting those secrets from their hiding places. In the process they venture far into dark, secluded canyons. They dig deep into the earth. They explore holes in the ground. And as some seek riches, others search for the mysterious. The unknown. The mythical.

Among these was a wild-eyed young man from Los Angeles who came to Death Valley in the late 1960s and pursued its mysteries and underground lore with a dark intensity that simultaneously thrilled and terrified his avid followers—most of them young women.

It was late in the summer of 1968 that thirty-three-year-old Charles Milles Manson came to Death Valley to check things out. The murderous events of the following summer had not yet been planned, and the so-called Manson "family" had not come here to hide from the police. Rather, the isolation of Barker Ranch—barely accessible via a tortuous trail up Goler Wash—offered just the sort of place Manson was seeking to bide his time when, as he insisted would happen soon, America's black population rose up against the whites. But even the remote Barker Ranch was not his ultimate hiding place; Manson believed in the depths of his mind that Death Valley was home to a secret door to the underground, and that this portal would be reached by descending through a flooded cave or hole or lake somewhere in the vast desert sink.

As Manson once explained to one member of his family, Charles "Tex" Watson, Death Valley was "a land where rivers ran upside down," a statement that dovetailed nicely with Manson's inverted sense of logic. In Watson's testimony regarding the soon to be famous Tate-LaBianca murders in the affluent foothill neighborhoods above Los Angeles, he elaborated on Manson's beliefs.

When we was in the desert the first time (1968), Charlie used to walk around in the desert and say—you see, there are places where water would come up to the top of the ground and then it would go down and there wouldn't be no more water, and then it would come up again and go down again. He would look at that and say, "There has got to be a hole somewhere, somewhere here, a big old lake." And it just really got far out, that there was a hole underneath there somewhere where you could drive a speedboat across it, a big underground city.

Much of what Charles Manson has been quoted as saying has been regarded as little more than LSD-induced fantasy. But the notion of a hole and underground lake in Death Valley is surprisingly close to being accurate, given that most of the water that flows into Death Valley does so underground. This includes the Amargosa River, which only occasionally surfaces for a short distance, then drops belowground again. Then there is Devil's Hole, which was believed by Manson to be one possible entrance to the lost city.

Manson's belief in a civilization beneath the desert also agreed with Hopi legends of "The Emergence," which tell of a hidden world beneath the desert where members of the Hopi Nation planned to hide if a catastrophe hit the earth, waiting to emerge when the fiery times were over. The Paiutes also retold ancient stories of underground cities and civilizations in the Death Valley region. And further linked to Manson's beliefs are stories from the early part of the twentieth century, one of them recounted in the 1932 book *Death Valley Men*, by writer and prospector Bourke Lee. Lee tells the story of two prospector friends of his—Jack and Bill—who, in the early '30s, were visited in their Emigrant Canyon cabin by two men in suits who said they had discovered a hidden passage beneath the bottom of a mine shaft. One of the suited men, Thomason, related the story to Jack and Bill as they listened in disbelief.

"My partner found it by accident. He was prospecting down on the lower edge of the range near Wingate Pass. He was working in the bottom of an old abandoned shaft when the bottom of the shaft fell out and landed him in a tunnel. We've explored the tunnel since. It's a natural tunnel like a big cave. It's over twenty miles long. It leads all through a great underground city; through the treasure vaults, the royal palace, and the council chambers; and it connects to a series of beautiful galleries with stone arches in the east slope of the Panamint Mountains. Those arches are like great big windows in the side of the mountain and they look right down on Death Valley. They're high above the valley now, but we believe that those entrances in the mountainside were used by the ancient people that built the city. They used to land their boats there."

"Boats!" demanded the astonished Bill, "boats in Death Valley?"

Jack choked and said, "Sure boats. There used to be a lake in Death Valley. I hear the fishing was fine."

Thomason next told them about the mummies he and his partner White had found in the cavernous city beneath the earth:

"The ancient people who built the city in the caverns under the mountain lived on in their treasure houses long after the lake in the valley dried up. How long we don't know. But the people we found in the caverns have been dead for thousands of years. Why! Those mummies alone are worth a million dollars!"

White, his eyes blazing, his body trembling, filled the little house with a vibrant voice on the edge of hysteria. "Gold!" he cried. "Gold spears! Gold shields! Gold statues! Jewelry! Thick gold bands on their arms! I found them! I fell into the underground city. There was an enormous room; big as this canyon. A hundred men were in it. Some were sitting around a polished table that was inlaid with gold and precious stones. Men stood around the walls of the room carrying shields and spears of solid gold. All the men—more than a hundred men—had on leather aprons, the finest kind of leather, soft and full of gold ornaments and jewels. They sat there and stood there with all that wealth around them. They are still there. They are all dead! And the gold, all that gold, and all those gems and jewels are all around them. All that gold and jewelry! Billions!"

The two prospectors watched out the door as Thomason and White departed. The visitors seemed to have no ulterior motives for concocting the story, for they asked nothing of the prospectors; there was no offer to the prospectors to join the expedition or request for them to help remove the gold or to contribute in any way toward the cause. According to Jack and Bill, the men named Thomason and White left as mysteriously as they had come.

A little more than fifteen years later, a *San Diego Union* newspaper article told of a retired Ohio doctor named Russell who claimed to have discovered relics of an ancient civilization, including mummies eight or nine feet tall, in the Death Valley region. According to local legend, Dr. Russell gathered a group of investors to remove the artifacts. They called their company Amazing Explorations, Inc. But on a trip to the site, Russell and his investors were unable to locate the entrance to the underground city. Not long after this, Russell's car was found abandoned in Death Valley. Russell was never seen again.

It would, of course, be easy to discount the above as wild tales concocted by grizzled prospectors and overzealous newspaper reporters. But the legend of an underground city has clearly persisted and continues to be retold today on a handful of Web sites, a few of which claim that Death Valley offers an entrance to the mythical city of Shambala.

Of course, if there truly were underground tunnels and chambers full of gold, not to mention ancient mummies and arched windows in the Panamints, it would seem likely that all of these would have been located and explored and featured on the Discovery Channel by now. But the very fact that the story persists tells us something about the mystique of Death Valley, the survival of mythology through the ages, and the desire in all of us to believe in the unbelievable. And I will admit without embarrassment that I, too, have stopped my car along the highway south of Furnace Creek and stared up at the two-mile-high wall of the Panamints, scanning the ancient cliff faces for signs of an opening.

⋇⋇⋇⋇⋇

If the holes in Death Valley are the stuff of lore and legend, so are the holes in space that have opened up on occasion to let in visitors from other galaxies—if a host of reports and witnesses and other purported evidence are to be believed.

One of the oldest sightings was made thousands of years ago by Indians who preserved what they had seen in petroglyphs. These ancient rock carvings seem to support Indian folklore that tells of two objects colliding high above Death Valley, with one of them crashing to earth. Supposedly the Indians observed a second craft landing near the first and helping to make repairs, and the two craft then launching back into the desert skies.

On August 19, 1949, two prospectors named Mace Garney and Buck Fitzgerald watched as a strange cylindrical object crashed in Death Valley. They guessed that it was about twenty-four feet across. The following day their story was printed in the local Bakersfield newspaper.

In November 1955, astronomer Frank Halstead, director of Darling Observatory in Duluth, Minnesota, was traveling to California with his wife, Ann, aboard a Union Pacific train. As they traveled along the outskirts of Death Valley, they caught sight of a strange cylindrical object.

"At first I thought the thing was a blimp—you know, one of those cigar-shaped dirigibles," said Halstead in a later interview. "But as I watched it, I realized that it could not be a blimp—they are only about two hundred feet long—and this thing was gigantic. It was about eight hundred feet long. I could estimate that because it was so close to the mountain range, where trees and clumps of trees were visible for comparison." Soon another object, a saucer-shaped craft, came behind the first. As Halstead and his wife looked on, both objects began to rise and eventually flew out of sight.

Nearly thirty-five years later, on a seemingly ordinary day in 1989, a UFO sighting was reported and another cylindrical object was captured in a photo above Death Valley.

If there indeed are holes in, around, or above Death Valley that lead to mysterious netherworlds, perhaps they offer one creative explanation for the many disappearances that have been recorded in the region over the past century and a half. During the late 1800s, when most of the serious mining operations were in business, miners and other laborers would now and again head off into the desert and never be heard from again. Most were assumed to have perished from heat or from falling off cliffs, dry waterfalls, or into unstable mining shafts. Because turkey vultures are known to pick apart dead bodies and coyotes haul off the remains, there were good explanations for the complete disappearance of people, and few major searches were ever launched. Others who disappeared were assumed to have been the victims of foul play. And some, no doubt, simply fled the region for cooler climes.

But in more recent times, the disappearances have continued. Early in 1986, Michael Keating, a man who lived in the Death Valley area and was known by many as Caveman Mike, took a walk out of a Saline Valley campground and was never seen again. Saline Valley is an isolated area of dunes and hot springs in the northwest part of Death Valley National Park. At the time of Keating's disappearance, the region was outside of national monument boundaries and thus experienced even fewer visitors than today.

In December 1986, less than a year after Caveman Mike disappeared, Barry Berman and his wife, Louise, both fifty-two, drove to Death Valley from Southern California. They camped at Saline Valley and, on the morning of January 6, apparently took a walk into the desert wearing tennis shoes, jeans, and thin shirts. Five days later, another camper reported to local law enforcement that the Bermans had not returned. Despite exhaustive searches, the two were never found.

In July 1996, in the midst of a record heat wave, four German tourists—a man and his eleven-year-old son, plus the man's girlfriend and her four-year-old son—were exploring Warm Spring Canyon and the abandoned Warm Spring mining camp, about twenty miles from the national park's isolated southern border. In August they were listed as missing. On October 21 their green Plymouth van was found bottomed out in nearby Anvil Spring Canyon. They were never found.

Is the entire region that surrounds Death Valley really somehow different from the rest of the Mojave Desert? Its geology and history are certainly more colorful. And the region has often seemed to be a magnet for people whose views on life are just a bit off center. But the site of untold riches and ancient civilizations? A hub of alien visitation? The truth, it would seem, remains elusive.

A Fateful Decision

JANUARY 15, 1850. Two weeks have passed and the mood about the small encampment is one of shared anticipation. All eyes scan the mountains. All ears listen intently for a distant whistle or war whoop. At any moment, salvation might appear in the form of two men trudging out of a nearby canyon or emerging like shimmering specters from the rolling waves of heat to the south. Each day begins and ends in silence as identical sunrises and sunsets parenthesize ten hours of waiting. Conversations are brief and no longer laced with futile attempts at optimism.

Near the third week of January, both Jean Arcane's and Asabel Bennett's teamsters decide to depart on foot.

"We bear you no ill will," Asabel tells the four men. "You signed on for the journey, but not for these circumstances. Take care and travel light. Perhaps we shall meet again somewhere in California."

But in his heart, Asabel knows he will never see them again. He knows they will perish long before reaching the fertile valleys and lush meadowlands of the Sacramento Valley. First, they will become separated, each taking his own trail as friendship fades and the instincts of survival take command. Not long after, one by one, the men will stop to scan the horizon for any signs of water. Then they will drop to the ground, thinking they need but a short rest before continuing. Finally they will close their eyes and pass into a gentle sleep; a sleep from which none of them will awaken. Over the next few months, their bodies will wither, their skin will toughen like leather, and eventually their bleached bones will litter the desert floor or decorate the sandy den of a coyote.

This is not all that Asabel knows. He knows that he himself will likely perish in the same manner. He knows this, yet, in some respects, it seems a great weight has been lifted from his shoulders. Suddenly the responsibility he feels for those in his party has been reassigned to fate, to the blowing wind, to the shifting sands and burning sun. Thus relieved of his burden, he can at last sit back and accept what befalls him. It is only the children he continues to worry about. Their sunken cheeks and lifeless eyes haunt his every waking hour. If it were possible to make a pact with Beelzebub himself, he would willingly forfeit his soul to ensure the childrens' safety.

A few days later, the Earhart brothers abandon their wagons and march north, followed by the two Alsatians. Then, early one morning, the Wade family departs in its wagon, heading south into the desert haze. Captain Culverwell follows on foot shortly after. Just two families—eight people—now remain in camp. And on a hot, windy afternoon more than three weeks from the day that William Lewis Manly and John Rogers left for help, Jean Arcane can no longer remain silent. Trudging over to Asabel Bennett's wagon, he stops short of the rig and calls him out from inside. Jean's fists are clenched and his face red with frustration.

"What is it, my friend?" asks Asabel, climbing down from his wagon.

"Our oxen can no longer support their yokes," Jean replies. "Each day they lose more weight. Their skin is abscessed and clings to their bones. Soon they'll not even be good for meat. We must leave now, Asabel! We must leave like the others. We must depart before we shrivel up as our livestock have and perish here!"

Asabel sighs and considers his response.

"I share your concerns, Jean," he says at length. "But our fate is no longer under our control. We have no choice but to wait. Tell me this: What if we set out on foot tomorrow and the boys show up the following day?"

Jean throws his hat to the ground. "Damn it, Asabel, we could carry that argument forward one day to the next without end! I ask you: What if we stay on, and they never return?"

Jean's wife approaches her husband and gently takes his arm. "Jean, dear," she says anxiously, "let's be civil and try to work this through."

"It's all right," Asabel tells her. "Jean has valid points; we should discuss them."

Jean retrieves his hat from the ground with a quick swipe of his hand. He studies the dusty brim, then looks up at Asabel, his anger in check for the moment. "Look," he says, "I'm willing to work through this but I want a plan. I'm weary of waiting here day after day with no alternatives but to wait."

Asabel pauses a moment before speaking.

"What if we were to stay a bit longer," he says, "but also prepare ourselves to leave at a minute's notice . . . should we have to."

"Ready ourselves to leave on foot?"

"Exactly," says Asabel. "The preparations would keep us occupied, and if Lewis and John have not returned by the date we set, we'll be ready to leave without the wagons."

"It's . . . a reasonable plan," Jean replies hesitantly, "but only if we can agree to a date. I will only wait so long for the boys to return, and I say we decide how long that will be—here and now!"

"How many days has it been already?" asks Sally Bennett, a tiny woman with a worried face. She has climbed down from the wagon to stand beside her husband.

Jean glances at the worn side-rail of his wagon, on which he has been carving a notch each morning since the two men departed.

"Twenty-two days," he says. "By my account, today is January 24."

"And what do you consider an appropriate time to wait?" asks Asabel.

"I should think two or three days would be more than enough," says Jean.

Asabel shakes his head. "It's not enough time," he says. "From the beginning, we were foolish to think they would be back in a few weeks. We were naive. We should have allowed a month or more. The distance they had to travel must have been far greater than any of us expected. We should have allowed for wrong turns or the possibility that the two would need to recuperate after reaching their destination."

"Hang it all, man!" shouts Jean. "Hundreds such allowances could be made! Where does speculation stop, and action begin?"

Frustrated, Jean walks over to stand beside his wife.

"Hear me, Asabel," he says, "I have never doubted a moment that Lewis and John would make every effort to return. I've never once questioned their integrity. But I have a wife and child here, as do you. All along, they have been my chief concern. You know as well as I that we could wait months, all the while making allowances for one delay or another until we have perished for lack of food. What happens when hot weather comes and this spring dries up? Then we shall have no food or water. I say two, maybe three days should allow for all possible delays and difficulties they might have encountered along their route."

"And I feel a few more weeks would be only prudent," Bennett replies.

Jean throws up his hands and turns to leave, but Abigail again takes his arm and stops him.

"Cannot the two of you compromise?" she asks hesitantly. "Could we not wait one more week before departing?"

Asabel looks at Jean sternly, then his face begins to soften.

"I suppose I could live with that," he says, "though my instincts tell me you're wrong."

Jean manages a brief smile. "All right, all right," he says. "I suppose I can manage another week if it means preserving our friendship."

They shake hands and agree to wait six days. During this time, preparations for departure will begin in earnest. Everything is to be made ready so they can move at a moment's notice, whether Manly and Rogers have returned or not. If by the morning of the seventh day, January 31, there is no sign of them, the Bennetts and Arcanes agree to head south with their families on foot.

Three-year-old Charley Arcane has come up behind his father and tugs on his coattails. "Will we have to walk a long way, Papa?" he asks.

"Not long, son," says his father, his eyes moist. "Soon we will be among the tall trees and green grass again. Above all else, you must believe this." And yet he is hard pressed to believe it himself.

Asabel and Jean now attend to the wagons, five in all counting the three abandoned by Earhart and Culverwell. Their plan is to salvage all usable materials, then abandon the rigs. First they remove the canvas covers, then help the women strip the material into smaller pieces to be sewn into breast straps, breeching, and five saddlebags for the remaining oxen. The same patient beasts who have pulled their wagons for more than a thousand miles will now be used as pack animals.

The women next empty their pillows of feathers to make use of the cloth cases. Other useful items are created by converting pieces of the wagons with one function into new items with totally different uses. Among these are leather moccasins that are stitched, then slipped over the bleeding hooves of the oxen.

When just three days remain before the deadline, their work has been completed and the two families return to a watchful stance. As they wait in silence, each man, woman, and child harbors his or her own secret fears and hopes as they sit in the shade of their wagons and watch the time pass.

Just after noon on January 30, 1850, the sound of a rifle shot cuts across the silent desert. The loud retort echoes against the mountains to the west, then fades back into silence. Jean Arcane, his wife, and their children have been asleep and are awakened by the noise, but don't know if it is a dream or an actual gun blast.

Unable to sleep, Asabel Bennett is first to crawl out from beneath his wagon, stand up, and look south down the valley. For several seconds he is silent as he focuses his eyes and tries to make out the images he sees in the distance. At length, with tears staining his dusty face, he raises his arms in the air and hollers loudly.

"The boys have come, the boys have come!"

Now the rest emerge slowly from beneath their skeletal wagons and rush up to greet the trail-weary figures of William Lewis Manly and John Rogers. Running as well as they can, Asabel and Sally Bennett catch Manly in their arms and fairly squeeze the life out of him. The Arcanes join them and vigorously shake Rogers's large hand, then Manly's when the Bennetts have finished with him. All the while, the children dance about the two men as if they are St. Nicholas and his helper come to bring Christmas gifts. Indeed, from his knapsack Manly retrieves four oranges and offers them to the children as presents. Noting Martha Bennett's weakened condition, he makes the other children promise to save one for the toddler.

"Surely, then, you have reached civilization," says Arcane, "for you have brought this fruit, and I see you have a donkey as well."

Standing beside Rogers is a little one-eyed mule, scraggly and gaunt, but loaded high with provisions and seeming to bear up well under his burden. Jean and Asabel help Manly and Rogers unload the beast, then they all walk back to the wagons to rest and hear a story of the long journey from which their two friends have at long last returned.

CHAPTER TEN

※

PUSHING IT TO THE EDGE

Adieu, adieu, kind friends, adieu,
I can no longer stay with you.
I'll hang my hat on a weeping willow tree,
And may the world go well with thee.

—REFRAIN FROM NINETEENTH-CENTURY BALLAD
"There Is a Tavern in the Town"

During my college years, when I departed L.A. for the University of Oregon, I wondered for a brief time if my Death Valley days might have come to an end. Rainy and gray for the better part of the year, the city of Eugene was a far cry from Southern California and I soon settled into a routine of dodging puddles, carrying textbooks in plastic bags, and learning to use such foreign devices as rubber boots and umbrellas.

Despite the change in scenery and weather, I carved out a niche for myself and befriended a number of other web-footed volunteers, most of whom hailed from the Northwest and were accustomed to large quantities of water falling from the sky. Still, I found three who were open to the idea of seeing the sun for a few weeks and so we decided to head south on the very first day of spring break.

Embarking on what would prove to be a frenetic and unexpectedly life-threatening trip for us all, we hit the road early one evening for an all-night driving session that, by midmorning of the following day, had taken us south through Grants Pass, Medford, and Ashland, across the Oregon border, and into Northern California lava country to connect with U.S. Highway 395 at the lonely outpost of Alturas. From here it was south to Susanville, past the depressing neon facades of Reno, then down that wildly beautiful stretch of road that curls around, then plummets over, the rim above Mono Lake.

At this viewpoint my three passengers were rewarded with the first real desertlike landscape they had ever seen. To celebrate the symbolic change in scenery, we pulled into a parking lot by the briny shores of Mono Lake and cracked open a six-pack of Coors we'd bought after crossing into California. (In those days you couldn't buy the stuff in Oregon.)

Mono is a troubled ecosystem, a dying 700,000-year-old lake that each year shrinks a little more while increasing in salinity. Too salty even for pupfish, its steel-gray waters support only brine shrimp and flies, which in turn attract large numbers of migratory waterfowl. Unfortunately the evaporation of the lake water has caused former islands to become peninsulas and the native birds that nest on these former islands are now exposed to coyotes and other predators. Meanwhile, the huge and grotesquely contorted spires and knobs of tufa, or calcium carbonate—formations that have lined the muddy lakeshore for centuries—have begun to collapse. This is in part because they are no longer exposed to the water that helped them grow. But it's also the result of pollution and vandalism.

The future of Mono Lake is somewhat brighter now that its cause has been championed by a number of ecological organizations. But back in those days the processes of damage had not become quite so noticeable and we, along with many others, were unaware of the controversies to come. At the time, we merely stood guzzling beers at the edge of the lake's alkaline shore while poking fun at a sign that said its waters were inhabited by "a brine shrimp."

"Just one?" exclaimed Jim Wagner, the red-haired, wild-eyed, bandanna-wearing hippie in our bunch. "Poor bastard must be lonely."

Heading south from Mono we passed through a big, wide-open landscape where everything was larger than life. To the west rose the craggy spires of the Sierras, home to Yosemite, Sequoia, and Kings Canyon National Parks—big-tree country. To the east the snowcapped wall of the White Mountains formed an equally imposing barricade. Accessible only a few months of each year, the highest peaks of this range are crowned with groves of ancient bristlecone pines. Twisted, gnarled, contorted with age, they are the oldest living things on earth.

Ahead of us lay the towns of Bishop, Big Pine, Independence, and Lone Pine, each little burg claiming to be the gateway to the Sierras and each consisting of a small strip of tackle shops, cafes, and small grocery stores. A boom of traffic and tourists and yuppies would begin to invade the east side of the mountains a decade later, but the trend had not yet begun at the time of our journey from Oregon. These were still sleepy little towns with a pleasant, unhurried feel to them. Protected from the populated west side of the state by the steep wall of the Sierras, the entire Bishop–Lone Pine corridor had remained essentially unchanged for decades. It was the sort of country a person might dream of disappearing to with a fishing pole and cooler, never to be heard from again.

But that was many years ago. The region's population has grown significantly in the meantime, especially in Bishop, where newly built hotels and restaurants and shopping malls and gift shops seem part of an attempt to upgrade the town's image, to establish the once rural byway as a trendy east-side destination. Thankfully, nobody has carved an east-west freeway through the Sierras, though I wouldn't be surprised if some bureaucrat in Sacramento or Washington, D.C., were mulling the idea over. If access to the region were ever made easier, the area would quickly become congested with thousands of west-side yuppies looking for someplace to experience the wilderness while enjoying latte grandes on the decks of their ten-room "rustic" retreats.

The little town of Lone Pine nestles on the shore of Owens Lake, the landmark sought so fervently by William Lewis Manly and company in the winter of 1850. This once pristine body of water has been mostly dry ever since a Los Angeles utility company strong-armed Owens Valley locals back in the 1940s into letting them tap the Sierra snowmelt that fed the lake. Now the sparkling mountain streams leave the slopes of 14,495-foot Mount Whitney and immediately enter a cement aqueduct that cuts south like a scar across the land for more than 250 miles. At its terminus, the water it carries meets up with the toilets and washing machines and swimming pools and dog dishes of Southern California.

State Highway 136, the road to Death Valley, departs Lone Pine just south of town, circles Owens Lake, passes the quasi–ghost town of Keeler, and follows the southern edge of the Inyo Mountains before joining State Highway 190. The road then scrambles over the northern foothills of the Argus Range, passes a viewpoint at Father Crowley Point, and descends into the saline trench called Panamint Valley.

After a quick stop at Indian Ranch to buy more beer, we climbed up into the rugged, largely treeless Panamint Mountains by way of Wildrose Canyon. Our only stop here was to pay homage to the cool and shadowy ruins of Wildrose

Station. Here, an eclectic mom-and-pop rest stop and concession stand had operated for years under a grove of sprawling cottonwoods. The place had originally been a stage stop around the turn of the twentieth century and, during the '30s, the buildings from a few nearby mining camps were moved here and immediately began exuding (free of charge) the irrepressible character of their original locales. Unfortunately, Wildrose Station was within monument boundaries and thus could not be left alone by the federal bureaucracy. Because it wasn't "up to code," the whole place was finally closed down and the buildings bulldozed in 1971, despite great public protest.

Shortly after our Wildrose pilgrimage, we were descending under darkening skies to Stovepipe Wells, our ears popping as we dropped from five thousand feet *above* sea level to some thirty feet *below*. Running late, we opted not to travel the additional thirty miles to the place we'd originally planned to camp. Instead, we decided to crash beside our rig in the Stovepipe Wells mobile home parking lot. How bad could one evening there be? The answer began to dawn upon us about 11:30 that night, as car after truck after camper after mobile home pulled into the lot, each aiming its headlights directly at our little makeshift campsite.

The reaction of my friends, who were expecting a wilderness camping experience, was swift and decisive. A middle-finger salute was offered by Don and John while Jim revealed a more creative side of his inner self to the arriving vehicles.

The next day we were up before dawn, grabbing a quick bath in the Stovepipe swimming pool, then heading off to explore the valley. First we trudged in a row along the ridges of the nearby sand dunes, hiking to the highest of the wind-rippled hills as we recited any lines we could remember from *Lawrence of Arabia*. Exploring cavernous Grotto Canyon came next, followed by a trip to Mosaic Canyon, with its slick, tilelike walls. Finally, as the sun hung low in the west, we headed up into the Marble and Cottonwood Canyons system, first driving and then hiking far into the hundreds-of-feet-deep, miles-long passageways until darkness fell like a blanket over us.

Sleeping under the stars near a crackling fire of dried mesquite branches has my vote as one of life's sweetest pleasures. Stuffed with medium-rare chuck steak, fried potatoes, and liberal quantities of screw-top wine, we lay on our backs and marveled at the closeness of the galaxy, the vastness of the desert, and the plaintive cries of a distant coyote.

"Life doesn't get much better than this," murmured Don before we all drifted off to sleep.

Next morning we took the highway east over a hump in the road called Daylight Pass, then around Corkscrew Mountain, briefly leaving Death Valley to gas up in Beatty, Nevada. The only attraction in Beatty back then was a small collection of dented Airstreams and faded, nondescript clapboard domiciles that (rumor had it) doubled as houses of ill repute. We were here, of course, to enjoy the *outdoor* scenery, but just knowing those Airstreams were there added an element of risk and excitement to our travels and provided incentive for some rather creative conversations to grow and flourish.

After gassing up, we fed our change to a few old slot machines and headed back down the highway, turning after a few miles onto a narrow dirt track that rose slowly to meet Rhyolite, a ghost town that had once been packed with more than twelve thousand townspeople. Back at the turn of the century, dozens of active mining operations had perched high atop the surrounding hills and a hundred or more stone and brick business structures stood proudly against the desert sky. A number of them had been bordellos and saloons, lending a somewhat bawdy and dangerous reputation to the town. But there also had been several water companies, an icehouse, hundreds of homes, a few churches, an opera house, two or three multistory bank buildings, and an elegant railroad station. Before the eventual collapse of the mines and demise of the town itself, Rhyolite boasted citywide telephone service and electric streetlights.

A few short decades later, most of the people had gone and nearly all the salvageable wood from homes and buildings had been removed. All that remains of Rhyolite today are a few dozen stone walls and foundations that continue to crumble under the effects of sun and sand and wind and rain. As for residents of the town, they have come and gone over the years—mostly gone. By the 1960s a mere handful of folks resided in the old train station and an adjoining railway car converted to an apartment. The last I heard, Rhyolite's newest residents were a group of gay activists whose intent was to revitalize the town, attract other gays and lesbians, and in the process perhaps restore the town's bawdy reputation. Very trendy of Rhyolite. What goes around comes around.

Southwest of Rhyolite, just a few miles before reaching Death Valley National Park, is the turnoff to Titus Canyon. This tight-walled, convoluted gash cuts a ragged course through the Grapevine Mountains before eventually descending an alluvial fan and entering Death Valley at its north end. The road through Titus has all the earmarks of a backdoor entrance. It's the flap at the rear of your long johns, the alleyway access to your favorite tavern. The moment you leave the highway, this one-way road wastes no time in rattling the bolts off your car and covering you with dust as you travel for miles across the sage-covered plain. You know the road is taking you somewhere because the mountains are growing nearer. At the same time you can't help but wonder if you've been caught in some sort of slo-mo time warp.

But that day we were granted a reprieve from the tedium of this interminable access road. A few miles before its ascent to the top of Bloody Gap, we encountered three jeeps and a group of college students poking about the vegetation with a graying, professorial type in khaki shorts and spectacles. Always up for some additional education, we pulled to a stop, got out, and shuffled over to audit the course.

"Death Valley, though usually considered a wasteland void of vegetation, is actually home to more than nine hundred species of plants," the professor was telling his students. "Of these," he added impressively, "more than twenty are found nowhere else in the world."

Among the plants he referred to that day were the Death Valley sandpaper plant, the Panamint daisy, and the Death Valley sage. If you know what you're looking for, you'll see them sprouting all over the valley and high up in the surrounding hills, healthy, happy, and thriving despite the adversities of summer sun, drying wind, and alkaline soil. But each year a handful of people will drive to Death Valley and other locations throughout the Mojave Desert, stop their car, raise the tailgate, pull out a shovel, and start digging up these and other native plants. They love the desert, they will tell you, and their aim is to re-create the arid environment in their backyards; a little bit of Mojave in Malibu. Their efforts, however, are almost always doomed to failure. Dig up these plants and take them home, give them rich soil and plenty of water, and they'll shrivel and die on you every time. Trying to transplant Death Valley vegetation is as foolish as trying to relocate one of the Lee brothers to New Jersey or move Salt Creek pupfish to the Pacific Ocean. In its patient and often incomprehensible way, nature has labored hard to provide an ideal place for everything and everybody. It is a scheme for living that is best left to unwind on its own without our interference.

Leaving the lecture with an incomplete, we climbed back in the car and continued on. Our plan was to spend the night in Leadfield, a ghost town that had been founded on deception of the cruelest kind. In 1925 and '26, a West Coast promoter posted billboards and ran advertisements in East Coast publications touting Leadfield as a booming metropolis on the banks of the Amargosa River. Fanciful drawings showed steamboats plying the river toward the thriving town. Unfortunately there *was* no town and the Amargosa was a prehistoric waterway that, for at least the last few centuries, has been intermittently dry or running underground for most of its sluggish course through the Nevada and California deserts. But never mind the hydrogeologic details; given the right sort of people—hopeful, naive souls who were willing to make a sizable real estate investment—the town was destined to become another St. Louis, or so the ads said.

Enticed by this pretty picture, nearly three hundred people parted with their cash, packed their belongings, and headed west. Lured by the thought of a fresh start, of a ground-floor opportunity, of a thriving community in which to live and raise their families, they crossed the Great Plains and Rocky Mountains, headed across the barren deserts of central Utah and southern Nevada, and descended at last into the rugged, steep-walled gash in the earth called Titus. And when they arrived, what they found was not a thriving city on the banks of a river, but two or three shacks perched precariously above a dry wash. They had been hoodwinked royally, but they were now out of funds and had no choice but to make a go of it at least temporarily. This the settlers did for several months, until they had exhausted their money, abandoned their dreams, and foreclosed on their hopes for a new life. Leadfield remains one of the few towns in the record books at which a post office opened and closed its doors in a single year.

To know its somber history makes the town's location seem all the more isolated, all the more desolate. Though Leadfield is just an hour up-canyon from Highway 190, it was clearly the end of the earth to those who settled here. Even today the few remaining cabins seem to sigh in the canyon winds, expelling the loneliness, lost dreams, and dwindling hopes that must have hung over the town like a layer of foul air. An aura of misfortune, the presence of disappointment, the remaining vapors of ruined lives and plans gone awry still seemed to lurk everywhere about the town that April as we followed a faint track leading out of the dry wash and parked up on a little raised bed of rock and gravel below the two or three remaining buildings. We would stay the night here, but none of us would sleep well; none of us would feel much at ease, each sensing the same *something* in the night air—something like unresolved anger, a simmering wrath, intangible, yet present as much as the rocks beneath our feet and the stars above our heads.

We left the next morning without cooking breakfast. Glad to be out of Leadfield, we negotiated the canyon's final tortuous narrows and followed the road as it broke free at last from the grip of the Grapevine Mountains and wound down the alluvial fan toward the simmering flats of Death Valley. Reaching the highway, we drove south toward Furnace Creek and spent the rest of the day hiking around the borax hills and shooting the breeze with employees at the visitor center.

Later that day we crossed the Devil's Golf Course via the West Side Road, a narrow wagon trail that was painstakingly carved through the beds of salt crystals by Chinese laborers in the early 1880s to accommodate borax wagons. On arriving at the foot of the Panamints, we drove south to visit Tule Spring and Bennett's Well. Both are brackish springs of water and historians feel that one or the other is likely the site of the camp where the Bennett-Arcane party stayed while William Lewis Manly and John Rogers went for help.

"The boys have come, the boys have come," I announced dramatically as we scanned the horizon like pioneers.

"Forget the boys," said John. "Did they bring any girls?"

Late that afternoon we drove up into the Panamints by way of Trail Canyon, a bitch of a wash through a rubble-strewn canyon that eventually morphs itself into a twisting, washboardy road. This in turn switchbacks its way up to Aguereberry Point, a 6,400-foot viewpoint accessible from Highway 190 when approached from the west. Of course, approaching anything by way of a paved road was too easy for the likes of us. We were seeking excitement and thrills and sore behinds, and this little stretch of one-mile-an-hour road was more than happy to accommodate. Unfortunately it grew dark well before we made it to the top; dark clouds had gathered by this time and a storm loomed to the north. When we at last reached a miner's shack perched high above the canyon, we read it as a sign that we should stop for the night. The windows of the shack were boarded up but the door was unlocked and could be secured against the coming storm, so we moved right in. Working hard to beat the rain, we hurriedly carried our campstove and lanterns inside, then hauled in our sleeping bags, the cooler of food, and the short case of Buckhorn beer we'd bought at the Furnace Creek Store. The luxury of drinking Coors had run its course; we now consumed whatever was cheapest.

The night we spent in this tin-roofed shack was much more satisfying than the one we'd passed in the cabin at Leadfield. The vibrations were more sympathetic here; someone had actually enjoyed life in this place. We all had a good night's sleep, disturbed only occasionally by the sound of kangaroo rats nibbling leftover crumbs from dinner and hopping across our chests to gnaw on our shirt buttons and pull at pieces of thread. Once during the night I awoke to the sound of a heavy rain splatting against the corrugated roofing. It was a comforting sound, one that meant wildflowers would bloom in the Mojave that year.

The final time I awoke, it was sometime before dawn and my ears were met by a deafening silence, the sort a person hears when the normally scheduled freight train fails to go by. I could tell that the rain had stopped, but as I listened intently, I began to detect a breezy sort of sound—a lot like the wind-through-the-trees noise you can hear with your hands cupped over your ears. Rising from my sleeping bag, I tiptoed to the door, intending to step outside and answer nature's call. Instead I was met with resistance from the other side; the door wouldn't budge. My thumping and knocking about eventually awoke Jim, who reluctantly left his sleeping bag and came over to help. With both of us putting our shoulders against the door, we at last forced it open.

To our surprise, we looked out to four inches of new-fallen snow and a layer of heavy slush that had blocked the door from opening. Dense, wet snowflakes collected in our hair and eyebrows as we gazed around us to see hills covered with white and tumbleweeds flocked like little round Christmas trees. Soon we were all up and running around in our shorts, heaving snowballs at each other. It would all be melted in a few hours, but it was a sign of a general trend that spring, a continuous onslaught of cool, unstable weather that would follow us for the next three days.

It also seemed to us that the rain and snow had come from the north, perhaps even from Oregon. Could it be that the clouds had found our hideout and were deliberately reminding us of our dwindling days down south and the responsibilities awaiting us back in Eugene? In those last few days, we visited a few more tourist spots, communed with nature in some out-of-the-way places I knew about, and more or less tried to follow the sun wherever it led us. One morning the four of us bounced up the alluvial fan to Echo Canyon, where we spent the next several hours exploring its twists and turns, climbing up to a natural arch high above the canyon floor, and poking around what was left of a little gold mining town called Schwaub.

I don't imagine there's much left in Schwaub these days. There wasn't a whole lot to it then, for that matter, though what remained was sufficient to stimulate my imagination and allow me to envision what life might have been like in this early twentieth-century mining town. I remember leaving the others to their explorations and sitting down by myself on the wood-planked porch of an old cabin that perched midway up a hillside above the town's main street. Here I was rewarded with a sweeping view of the canyon, the town's scattered cabins and storage sheds, the old stamp mill, and the timbered entrances to five or six mine tunnels dug right into the surrounding canyon walls.

A little way below me lay the rusted body of a Model T car. Roofless, motorless, and half buried in sand, it clearly wasn't going anywhere soon. But as I gazed down at the car, I swore I could hear the engine start to hum and rattle as it clanked its way down-canyon toward Furnace Creek. I couldn't make out who was driving, perhaps the owner of the mine or maybe a mill worker going for supplies. To my right, the twisted handlebars and seat springs of an old tricycle, upside down, lay amidst a pile of rusted tin cans and broken bottles. It hadn't been ridden in decades, but in my mind I imagined the figure of a four-year-old boy pedaling that tricycle furiously in circles around the covered porch on which I sat. The face of the toddler was flushed with a combination of pride and simple exertion; his curly red hair rustled about his face in the breeze of his own making. Inside the cabin and leaning out through the paneless window frame stood his auburn-haired mother, her careworn face aged beyond her years but her smile reflecting her love for that child, her one ray of hope in a harsh and uncertain life.

Because so many of these mining towns sprang up overnight and were abandoned nearly as quickly, it's often difficult to get a clear picture of the street layout or the day-to-day activities that went on here. Like most small, forgotten desert towns, Schwaub is quiet and empty; it holds its secrets close to its heart. Still, there must be memories lying just beneath the sand or hovering just above the town, blown about by little gusts of wind that now and again rattle through the sheets of metal roofing. I like to think that if I'm quiet and patient, such memories will float through the air and pass through my head and the town will spring to life—if only momentarily—before returning to silence.

It was inevitable that Friday would come. With just twelve more hours to explore Death Valley, we decided to travel north to Scotty's Castle, then west to the Racetrack, leaving Death Valley by way of a reasonably good jeep road that passed by both Ubehebe Peak and Hunter Mountain. I'd been this way before and felt it would make for a fitting conclusion to our trip.

We spent several hours at the Racetrack, wandering around the lake bed made famous by its mysterious moving rocks, pacing off the distance of tracks, and looking for the largest boulders on the playa bed. From the edge of the lake we spotted some burros high in the hills above and watched a vulture circle a nearby canyon before finally dropping out of sight as it homed in on its prey. At our feet, a tarantula wandered out from under a bush and we watched it scurry across the rocky earth as if late for an appointment.

We reluctantly clambered back into the Land Cruiser and resumed our trip. Soon we left the desert terrain behind and, at about seven thousand feet in elevation, scrub pine and junipers became the trees of natural selection. As we climbed we also began to encounter snow along the road; before long the white stuff began to cover the dirt track itself. In four-wheel drive and low gear, I had no problem plowing through the light cover of snow, but as we approached a series of switchbacks that hung above a steep-walled canyon, I worried for the first time that the way ahead might be impassable. There was less than a mile of road in front of us before we'd begin losing elevation again; if we could make it that far, we'd probably be all right. But there was a good six-inch base of snow on the road now and the new stuff on top was slushy and hard to track through.

A few times I felt the rear wheels slip and our rig begin to slide toward the edge, only to feel them grab again and straighten us out. Along one especially narrow section, we approached a spot where a chunk of the road had collapsed and fallen into the canyon. As I hugged the wall of earth on my right to edge the car around this big divot, I scraped the side with the right-hand mirror as we passed. Looking in the rearview mirror, I watched a little flurry of rocks tumble down across the road. At last we rounded a bend and turned away from the cliff. I sighed audibly as we left the canyon behind and began to climb through a thick grove of stunted junipers and into a landscape of little tree-covered knolls and immense snow-covered boulders.

Just as I began to think the worst was over, we slid around a bend and ran smack into a drift of snow about two feet deep and twenty feet long. There was no going around it and certainly no going over it. Our only choice was to clear the bulk of the snow away. "No sweat," somebody said, so we stopped the car and pulled out our one small shovel. We worked for a good hour, taking turns at clearing a path as daylight waned and a light sleet began to fall. As the last shovels of snow were flung out of the way, I flipped on the headlights; the way ahead was growing dim.

To this day I'm not quite sure why we put in all this effort without first hiking up the road to see what might lay ahead. I suppose it seemed easier to tackle our immediate problems without looking for more around the bend. Our success, however, was short-lived. A few more turns in the road brought us to a drift even deeper than the first; this one stretched out a good forty feet or so. By this time the sun had truly set and we were in no shape for any more strenuous digging. Reluctantly we decided we'd have to turn back.

Unfortunately this meant driving all the way back down to Stovepipe Wells, then back up over Towne Pass via Highway 190—all told, a 140-mile detour from our planned route. Worse, we'd have to back down the first mile or so until we reached a wide spot just before the stretch of canyon. A sense of panic came over me as I considered what lay before us. Backing a car down a winding canyon road would be challenging enough, but at night and with slick snow covering the road, the prospects were frightening to consider. Still, as long as I could tackle this thing methodically—slowly and carefully—I figured I could get through it.

The first half-mile was a breeze. Except for an occasional spinning wheel, I managed to backtrack pretty well. We made it as far as the first switchback around the canyon before I felt I was losing control. Here, the road had either been banked improperly or perhaps it was decades of erosion at work; whatever the case, the road surface sloped toward the canyon rather than away from it. As much as I tried to hug the walls of the inside bank, I felt the same helpless feeling a person experiences in one of those fun-house rooms with crazily sloping floors, steeply angled walls, and no reference marks for gaining perspective. In this case the road served as the fun-house floor; the only things approximating walls were the steeply pitched angles and drop-offs of the canyon below. Adding to the whole topsy-turvy effect was the steadily falling snow, which had picked up considerably and now drove at the windows at a nearly horizontal angle. This further eroded any sense of perspective, judgment of distance, line of horizon, or direction of retreat.

But retreat we did, slowly, almost imperceptibly at some points where visibility was so bad that we slowed to a crawl. By this time, my passengers' words of support had crumbled into exclamations like "Shit oh dear," "We're going over the fucking edge!" and "I could be in Eugene drinking beer right now!"

These brief outbursts were our feeble attempts to manage the situation, to control the uncontrollable. But the road was clearly in control of us. All the holes and divots and fallen rocks we had easily avoided in the daylight now began to stalk us from behind, grabbing our tires as we backed over them, throwing us off our seats, jerking the steering wheel out of my hands, and pulling us into slides and turns and sickening spins we had no way of avoiding. The climax came when we hit a patch of ice and began to skate slowly—almost gracefully—toward the edge of the road.

Far below, the canyon floor was lost in a mist of cloud and snow. But each of us knew what awaited us there—a hundred-foot drop to a sandy wash littered with boulders and brush and rusted beer cans and shattered pop bottles. Strangely, as we slid toward the edge, I found myself envisioning the collection of items we would soon join. A Nesbitt's bottle from the '50s caught in the arms of a dwarf piñon pine. A Bud Light can of contemporary vintage wedged between two boulders from the Ordovician period. An eclectic jumble of old and new, natural and man-made, coexisting in perfect harmony.

Shaking myself from my daze, I stared through the steamy window and tried to focus on the side mirror. In it I saw a reflection of the left rear wheel sliding sideways toward the huge divot we had earlier avoided. Hitting the brakes seemed a foolish move; in doing this I would only succeed in locking the other three wheels as well. But to do nothing—to let the car slide off the road and down into the foggy void—was no option. If I turned the wheel I might pull out of the skid, but I knew that only a small amount of control could ever be regained once a car began to slide.

The most frightening aspect of this whole incident was the deliberate, almost methodical movements of the vehicle and the seemingly endless length of time that passed. Though my life may not have flashed before my eyes, the prospects of its ending surely did. Intensifying the effect were the curses, shouts, and cries that came from my fellow riders—agitated noises that merged into the frantic, pizzicato sound track to some macabre horror film. But neither my fragmented thoughts nor the erratic comments of my passengers had any effect as the rear of the vehicle drew ever nearer the edge.

It was a small rock that stopped our slide. An insignificant piece of rubble. Because the vehicle had continued to creep slowly backward as its rear end was simultaneously sliding sideways, the wheels continued to encounter new road surface and, at a moment that was nothing short of apocalyptic, the left rear wheel slid into the rock and came to a momentary halt. At this point it seemed safe to tap the brakes. And as I did so, the rock was jarred to life and it clattered over the edge and into the mist below.

We sat for several seconds at the edge of this drop-off, a collective sigh issuing forth. This was quickly followed by a rash of good-for-any-occasion swear words. Then I carefully slid the vehicle into first gear and pulled slowly forward until we had moved away from the edge. Maneuvering as near to the opposite bank as possible, I continued backing, this time with no further incidents. When at last we reached the wide spot in the road, I turned the car around and we continued down the mountain. Several moments of silence followed as each of us assessed our recent brush with death. Finally one of us, I think it was Jim Wagner, offered a sage and fitting remark.

"Good-*fucking*-bye, Death Valley."

As we dropped below the snow line and rolled on down toward the Racetrack, the panic was over and our minds and bodies eventually resumed operation. But hours later, as we flew down the highway with Death Valley behind us, I couldn't help but wonder in silence about the suddenness of circumstance and the steadfast disinterest of the earth in we fools who scuttle across it. Nor could I stop puzzling over it being a rock that had saved us. A small rock we had earlier dislodged when the mirror had brushed against a bank of earth. In the end, we had been saved from our own stupidity by a small piece of the earth that had likely spent its lifetime in a single spot until we knocked it out of place. A rock that had rolled to the edge of the road and waited in the precise spot where we would need it to be.

A warning, perhaps? A reprieve by God or nature? Or had it been a mere fluke, a chance occurrence, dumb luck? Whatever the source and significance of our salvation, I would accept the offering with grace and humility.

CHAPTER ELEVEN

BURROVILLE

ME LONELY? HELL NO! I'M HALF COYOTE,
HALF WILD BURRO!

—BALLARAT CEMETERY HEADSTONE OF CHARLES FERGE
("SELDOM SEEN SLIM"), 1889–1968

Many years ago, I was loosely affiliated with a group of desert hikers who had this crazy idea of mapping a desert trail from the Mexican to the Canadian border. The goal was to create an arid-lands version of the Pacific Crest Trail, and the Desert Trail Association needed volunteers to try out various routes and report back on accessibility, ease or difficulty of passage, scenic highlights, and availability of water.

Because I thought the Racetrack might be an interesting sight for hikers to visit during treks through the desert, I took it upon myself to see if it was possible to hike all the way from the floor of Death Valley to Racetrack Valley by way of the Marble and Cottonwood Canyons complex. Don't sweat the geography: The point was that if a person couldn't easily hike from east to west to reach the Racetrack, it would mean a major detour from the main trail and would be well out of any hiker's way.

And so, armed to the teeth with all the potatoes and beef jerky and oranges and six-packs of Buckhorn I could squeeze into my pack, I bounced on up the washboard road to the Racetrack early one spring morning. Parking my rig near the mouth of the most impressive canyon leading up into the Panamints, I made camp for the night. The next morning I planned to get an early start and use my trusty USGS map to chart a course up into the mountains and down through the canyons into Death Valley. With any luck I'd arrive in a day or two at Stovepipe Wells, just in time for happy hour and a hearty round of applause by the tavern regulars.

I spent a cool and starry night at the Racetrack. It was also a noisy night, for the coyotes were full of romance or loneliness or whatever else it is that makes them howl their heads off. Eventually I drifted off to sleep and dreamed I was leading a 1920 archaeological expedition across the Gobi Desert.

At first light I jumped out of my bag, fried up a potato, washed it down with a warm beer, and started my trek up the alluvial fan leading into the unnamed canyon ahead of me. Of course, it would no longer be unnamed once I had charted my route through it. But what should I call the place, I wondered. Something with my own name in it? John's Gap? Soennichsen Gulch? Or perhaps something more historical and in line with the surrounding topography. Something like Crack-o'-Day Canyon or Arroyo Grande?

After an hour of hiking I reached the entrance to a wide wash that continued for about a mile ahead of me before pulling to the right and out of sight behind the steadily rising canyon walls. As I made my way deeper into the shadows, the bray of a burro somewhere ahead told me I wasn't alone.

At one time populating the Panamints and surrounding mountains by the thousands, Death Valley's burros are descendants of the pack animals owned by hundreds of prospectors who poked around this region during the late nineteenth and early twentieth centuries. Innately suspicious and often standoffish, these wild offspring will nevertheless approach tourists now and then to sample their Oreos or ham sandwiches or gummy bears. Mostly, though, you'll only see signs of their passing, not the animals themselves.

The name *burro* is simply Spanish for *donkey*. Because the early Spanish explorers discovered and occupied lands that were chiefly west of the Mississippi, the name *burro* is still used in the western half of the United States while *donkey* is employed in central and eastern parts of the country. The burros found in America today are thought to be descendants of those brought and bred here by the Spanish conquistadors in the sixteenth century. Going back much farther, the burro's likely ancestor was the Nubian subspecies of African wild ass. The ass, or donkey, was important as a pack animal in ancient Egypt, perhaps more so than the ubiquitous camel usually associated with Egyptian civilization. In the Holy Lands, they were the most common beast of burden and the chosen mode of transportation for the poorer classes. The donkey has a cameo role in the Ten Commandments, and Jesus is said to have ridden a donkey into Jerusalem.

It is thought that the first donkeys in Europe came by way of a supply ship during the second millennium BC. More than thirty-five centuries would pass until the animals were shipped to America as part of Christopher Columbus's cargo on his second trip to America in 1495. The four jacks and two jennies that trotted down the ramp onto the docks at the Hispaniola port would eventually produce mules and hinnys for the conquistadors' subsequent expeditions throughout western North America. (Mules are the result of a male donkey mating with a female horse; a hinny is produced by a female donkey and male horse).

The arrival of burros in the western United States was due almost exclusively to the California gold rush, during which a disproportionately large number of the earliest prospectors were Mexican. Almost overnight, the image of the solitary, grizzled prospector and his beloved burro became synonymous with the gold rush and Old West vignettes found in newspaper stories, dime novels, paintings, and songs of that era. But burros were not owned solely by the single-blanket prospectors. As the years passed and mining operations became larger and more complex, the animals increasingly were used to haul provisions to mining camps, pull carts of ore and debris from mine tunnels, and carry rough ore to the mills. There, other burros were employed to walk in circles and turn the wheels that crushed the ore.

The legacy of burros in Death Valley is a fascinating one. It seems likely that the first burro to enter the valley was a little fellow named Ol' One Eye, who carried supplies for William Lewis Manly and John Rogers on their return trip to rescue members of the Bennett and Arcane families from Death Valley in January 1850. The burro, given to the men by Mexican ranchers who had nursed them back to health, accompanied Manly and Rogers back from the San Fernando Valley to Death Valley via the same tortuous route they took through the Panamint Mountains. Ol' One Eye put up with a lot on this trip. They had to lower him down and later winch him back up over a dry fall in the canyon they passed through to reach the valley floor. They loaded him down with supplies and he was also ridden now and again by party members who were too sick or sore to walk. It would be nice to think that this stalwart fellow is the great ancestor of all future burros in Death Valley, but this is not the case, for Ol' One Eye left the valley and made his way back to civilization with the rescued '49ers. I like to think he was led out into a green pasture to spend the rest of his days eating bunch grass and tortillas.

The true ancestors of today's Death Valley burros arrived with the first prospectors who came to seek their fortune. The prospectors journeyed to the deep saline trench after hearing tales of gold and silver that had begun to circulate a few years following the arrival in Southern California of the ragtag remnants of the Jayhawker and Bennett-Arcane parties. This was in the mid-1850s and did not produce a flood of prospectors, but a handful here and there, tentatively setting foot along the edges of the great sink and looking for telltale veins in the walls of Panamint canyons, the alluvial washes of the Funeral range, and at dozens of other unnamed, unmapped places in this vast desert region.

The single-blanket, jackass prospectors, as they were called, explored the Death Valley area in ever growing numbers for the remainder of the nineteenth century. In their solitary endeavors, their burros became their pets, their best friends. In early tintypes and later photographs, it was rare to see the prospector without his trusty burro standing patiently by his side. Also attesting to the burros' importance, newspapers frequently mentioned them in stories about lost or injured miners.

Rhyolite Herald, June 16, 1905

PERISHED IN DEATH VALLEY

Prospectors crossing Death Valley have recently found three dead burros; which died in the harness. The burros were packed with provisions, etc., and without doubt belong to some prospector who may have met a similar fate. Lack of water was the probable cause.

The Tonopah Bonanza, July 1909

For the first time in history so far as anyone is able to learn, a terrible storm has swept Death valley, leaving ruin and desolation in its wake.

Yesterday the news was received in Tonopah of the severest storm that has ever occurred in that region of utter desolation so far as vegetation and the such are concerned. From what details could be learned, prospectors were racing for their lives to places of safety. Burros have been rendering the days and nights hideous with their pitiful wails and many have met death.

As with other regions of California, mining companies formed in Death Valley and a few towns were put together. All regarded the burro as integral to their operations, and the animals flourished here in the desert heat that mimicked their ancestral African homelands. And when the borax boom of the 1880s led to a major operation at the Harmony Borax Works on the valley floor, it wasn't long before the value of the burros' hybrid relatives became even more appreciated. The nearest railroad in those days was at Mojave, 165 miles away. It was clear that wagons would be needed to cart the raw borax crystals to the railroad town, but what animals should be used? Horses? Oxen? Burros? Mules?

It was determined by 1884 that mules would be best, since they combined the sure-footedness of burros with the intelligence and temperament of horses. A Harmony Borax Company foreman purchased a team of eight mules along with another team of twelve that had been used for a previous borax operation. Harmony Borax also hired a man named Ed Stiles, who had been driving the team of twelve.

It didn't take long for the foreman to see that a team of twelve mules could haul twice the load of a team of eight. Could it be that each time a mule team was increased by 50 percent, the productivity doubled? Putting his premise to the test, the foreman connected the team of eight to the team of twelve, and although the whole outfit—including two ore wagons, a water wagon, and twenty mules—stretched out for more than one hundred feet, his theory was proven true. All that was needed now was a new, sturdier sort of wagon that would hold nearly five thousand pounds of borax, travel easily over rock-strewn, steeply sloping ground, and operate as trouble-free as possible. The end result was the now-famous twenty-mule-team wagons that eventually became the corporate symbol for the U.S. Borax Company. There was more to be done than training mules and building wagons, however. A road needed to be hacked through the vast bed of salt spires known as the Devil's Golf Course. Chinese laborers toiled for months until an eight-mile-long, six-foot-wide passage had been broken through the salt field.

Handling the team of mules was a skill not easily earned. The mules themselves had to learn techniques such as "jumping the chain" to exert a force at an angle to other mules in the team, allowing the whole affair of mules and wagons to round sharp turns safely. Early on, it was determined that the first two animals should be strong draft horses rather than mules, so the term "twenty-mule team" has always been somewhat of a misnomer. But the unique wagon designs, the shared isolation and incredible teamwork of the men who operated the teams, and the legacy of the sure-footed little beasts themselves have become legendary. The design and construction of the wagons proved to be as incredibly reliable as intended; during the five years the wagons hauled borax on a daily basis—from 1885 to 1890—they transported an estimated 2.5 million pounds annually, never once breaking down.

It should be noted that when new U.S. Borax Company owner F. M. Smith observed mules hauling borax wagons in 1894, he determined that a more modern system should be employed at the company's Borate, California, operations. The result was the purchase and modification of a huge three-wheeled tractor that burned one and a half tons of coal a day and chugged up grades in a manner that drivers compared to "climbing a bar of soap." After just one year, Smith reluctantly approved returning to mule power.

The age of both mules and burros, however, was about over in California. Around the same time that California's goldfields were just about tapped out, the railroad made its way to the western states. Almost overnight, the long-cherished burros lost their significance as transportation and pack animals. And quickly following this sudden devaluation, they began to be abandoned by their former owners.

It took longer in Death Valley, where the search for gold had not been prompted by a single major discovery like that at Sutter's Mill in Northern California. It was a slow and steady process that brought people into and then back out of this extreme part of the Mojave. The burros of Death Valley, along with their cousins the mules, had a rich history of service for more than sixty years—longer if we accept those few single-blanket prospectors who lingered on into the 1930s and '40s, throwbacks to an earlier era.

Eventually the mountain ranges flanking Death Valley were empty of prospectors and filled with free-roaming descendants of those first trailblazing animals from the 1850s. Moreover, they were becoming as much of an attraction to the growing tourist trade as were the geologic wonders of Death Valley or the elegant suites and gourmet banquets at the Furnace Creek Inn, a luxury hotel completed in 1935 by the Pacific Coast Borax Company.

Unfortunately the burros of Death Valley had adapted so well to their desert home that by the 1950s and '60s they increasingly became the focus of government efforts to remove them from the region. Competition with bighorn sheep, desert tortoises, and other native mammals for sparse vegetation and limited water was generally cited as the reason for removing them. Removal techniques included relocation, adoption, and .45-caliber bullets.

Fortunately the Wild and Free-Roaming Horse and Burro Act of 1971 pretty much eliminated euthanasia as a means of removing burros and horses from federal lands. The policy of the National Park Service is now one of removal and adoption of burros it determines to exceed a number that will not threaten native species. The debate continues as to the sometimes conflicting goals of protecting native species and preserving the historical legacy of places like Death Valley, a legacy that most certainly includes our friends, the burros. For many of us, they are as much a part of the landscape here as salt flats, alluvial fans, and abandoned mine buildings.

And on that sunny May morning, they were about to be a part of *my* landscape and in numbers too great to be ignored. It was after about two hours of hiking up the rock-strewn wash and rounding a bend in the canyon that I entered Burroville—population about a hundred, if my head count was accurate. The majority of them stood in little groups all over the surrounding talus slopes; several more perched even higher atop the perpendicular cliff walls. From their various vantage points, the lot of them were motionless as the stones beneath their feet. And all stared hard at me as I cautiously entered their canyon domain.

Not much farther up the wash, I encountered an imposing welcoming committee—a dozen big jacks with massive heads, standing shoulder to shoulder ahead of me in the wash and daring me to approach. Though they stood a good thirty feet away, their resolute stance and effective blockade of the canyon ahead made me pause a good long time to consider my next move. I'd never heard of anyone being attacked or killed by a burro, but it was clear they had no plans to move or let me pass.

Several moments went by while I considered whether to lob a few potatoes at them, scream loudly and wave my hands, or simply wait until they had tired of standing there. At last one of the jacks pawed at the ground with his hooves and another looked behind him, as if to check for a surprise attack. That's when I saw what the burro was actually looking at—a jenny and nursing foal standing close beside the canyon wall about twenty feet behind him. Her flanks shuddered and her tail switched as she watched me with a wariness only a wild animal can display. Then, as my eyes scanned the steep slopes behind her, I began to pick out other females and their young, planted in groups of two and three all around me. Now I began to understand that it was the time of year for colts to drop, and the big males were merely protecting the herd. I must have let out a big sigh about this time, because one of them pricked up his ears and raised his head as if waiting for me to speak.

"Don't worry, guys, I'm just passing through," I called gently.

No response, just a flutter of flanks and a few ear twitches. Clearly the subtle approach wasn't working, so I picked up a rock and lobbed it at the biggest jack. It fell at his feet and he lowered his head to sniff at it.

"That's right," I thought to myself. "The smell of man: time to back off and let me pass."

But the big jack's nose merely nudged the rock forward a few inches and he snorted at it, raising a small puff of dust. After staring at the burros for a long time, I looked up again at all the little clusters of them dotting the cliffs around me. Then it slowly dawned on me that I was the alien here; I was the intruder. Could I really blame them for patrolling their own neighborhood? Hardly. It also seemed clear by now that they had no intention of moving, so I reluctantly turned around and began to make my way back down the wash in defeat. That was when a loud bray made me about-face once more. To my surprise the big jacks were now lumbering out of the wash toward the northern walls of the canyon. The biggest of them had paused at the edge of the wash bank and was staring right at me.

Suddenly the way was clear; I'd won the standoff. And yet as I again considered making my way up-canyon, I looked up at the burro's smoky muzzle and my gaze was suddenly confronted by his own great brown eyes. And as we stood there staring at each other, some thirty feet apart at the entrance to this narrow desert canyon, a shudder passed through me.

It has been my experience that humans, as a rule, tend to look past, or even right through, the eyes of animals. The wall that nature has erected between species is broad and high, yet I've always imagined that we have the ability to scale that wall or bore through it if only we allow ourselves to be sympathetic to the phenomenon. When conditions are ideal, I believe we all have the chance to experience a sense of understanding that passes between man and animal through direct, intentional eye-to-eye contact. This understanding can manifest itself in many emotional messages: the terror of a doe in the sight of a gun, the rage of a injured dog in a dark alleyway, the abject misery of an aged baboon in a zoo enclosure—whatever the unspoken message, it manages to momentarily leap the biological gap between species and offer a transient opportunity for two minds to meet when dialogue is impossible.

All this happened to me that day as the burro's dark eyes found my mine and I encountered his. The message he sent to me there in that rocky wash bed became clear: I was being asked to leave the canyon. Politely, and with some measure of supplication, but succinctly—plain as day. And I knew I couldn't go on, couldn't violate his trust. Not now. So I slowly turned and headed back down-canyon toward the Racetrack.

I began to consider my role in helping to create a desert trail that dozens, possibly hundreds, of hikers would traverse each year. Today's unknown route through a rugged canyon might well become a dotted red line on some future map. Was it really so important, I wondered, that people know about and pass through this place? I was beginning to realize it wasn't. Hell, I muttered to myself, maybe what this earth really needs is a few more unnamed canyons. Maybe there's an intrinsic value in knowing that some mountains will never be climbed, that a handful of jungles will remain unexplored, that a few oddities of nature will forever escape discovery or—if discovered, like the Racetrack—will never be *fully* understood.

Could it be that as our world shrinks around us and fewer and fewer untamed regions are left, each of these remaining areas of pristine purity, of stark beauty, of unexplained phenomena somehow take on an aura of greatness, of specialness, of holiness? Might it be that the very *existence* of undiscovered country, of untamed wilderness, of unanswered riddles is what makes our populated places livable, our urban lives more tolerable? And if this is so, must we really clamber up every alluvial fan, map every desert canyon, and slap a name on every mountain peak and dry lake and rocky outcropping?

Perhaps, in the end, it's enough just knowing they're out there.

CHAPTER TWELVE

CHASING A SPIRIT

You can't see anything from a car; you've got to get out of the god-damned contraption and walk, better yet crawl, on hands and knees, over the sandstone and through the thornbrush and cactus. When traces of blood begin to mark your trail you'll see something, maybe. Probably not.

—EDWARD ABBEY,
Desert Solitaire, 1967

For a brief time in the early 1980s, a whirlwind of contro-versy swirled around Death Valley administrators, visitors, geologists, and other concerned parties, each of whom main-tained a slightly differing stance on what should be done to save a park attraction called Mushroom Rock.

To me it had always looked more like a withered stalk of broccoli, but the chunk of soot-colored lava had nevertheless garnered a small following over the years as it squatted just five or six yards off the highway south of the visitor center. In the gift shop, colorful postcards portrayed the rock from an assortment of angles, as did tiny peephole slide viewers made in Korea and key chains and bright-red felt pennants shouting "Death Valley '49ers!" as if this were the home of an NCAA football team.

But as the souvenirs were hawked, the rain, wind, sun, and sand were steadily eating away at Mushroom Rock, just as they'd been doing for thousands of years. Now the formation teetered precariously atop its slender base, threatening to topple with the next good windstorm or poorly executed left turn by the myopic driver of a late-model Chrysler Imperial.

Among the proposals to save the rock were a suggestion to coat its base with a resinous cement mixture, a plan for covering it with a huge plastic dome, and a complex idea utilizing metal reinforcing rods as a sort of high-tech brace to keep it standing upright. As all these proposals were being offered, a few Sierra Club types were so brash as to suggest that the gradual demise of the rock was a natural process and should be allowed to continue.

When all is said and forgotten, the furor over Mushroom Rock was really much ado about nothing. True, the volcanic oddity had been mentioned by writer John Spears way back in 1891 and had obviously been around quite a while before that, but it wasn't all *that* old, geologically speaking. It wasn't even unique; thousands of infinitely more curious rock formations exist all over the country.

So why was it so popular? First, unlike a desert sunset or approaching sandstorm or the pungent odor of burning mesquite, the rock was a tangible object, a physical landmark visitors could say they had seen, touched, and stood beside while posing for the camera. Second, it was right along the main highway, at an ideal spot for tourists to visit without actually stepping out of their car. It was, in other words, *accessible*, thus fitting in nicely with a few dozen other attractions in Death Valley that can be visited with a minimum of energy expended.

Like Mushroom Rock, several other places in Death Valley have been given clever names, among them the Devil's Cornfield, Artist's Palette, and Twenty-Mule-Team Canyon. Never mind that the cornfield is a small patch of arrowweed stalks and the palette is an eroded hillside with a few pastel variances due to mineral content. And disregard the fact that not a single one of the famous twenty-mule-team wagons ever rolled through Twenty-Mule-Team Canyon.

Clearly these sites have become popular destinations because visitors can view them quickly, safely, and without leaving their automobiles. As a model of efficiency, the system works surprisingly well; nearly a million tourists visit Death Valley each year, traveling up and down the three hundred miles of paved roads before departing to make room for the next batch of tourists.

Those who choose to stay in the area for a few days or more can check into a four-star hotel, a modest motel room, or one of a handful of rustic cabins (*rustic* meaning a lengthier hike to the ice machine). The more adventurous visitors who have chosen to haul their homes along with them are diverted into a massive parking area that has been bulldozed, graded, subdivided, numbered, patrolled, and regulated for their safety, convenience, and comfort. On a busy day in November, the glint of sun on sheet metal is resplendent.

Whenever I used to see long lines of cars and motor homes passing in both directions along the main Death Valley highways, I couldn't help but think of ants scurrying along a two-way trail to and from their anthill. Dutifully tending to their communal business, they move steadily along in the efficient pursuit of their predetermined objectives for the day. But far more interesting to me, as an observer, is the ant that strays off the beaten path and spends his time poking around in the underbrush a few feet off the main thoroughfare.

To be sure, we are all different and each of us has his or her own way of experiencing nature; I certainly have no desire to attempt the conversion of satisfied tourists who number in the millions. My only dismay comes from knowing that so many people are unable to take that leap; unable to separate the rewards of urban pleasures from those derived through interactions with the natural world. I enjoy steak and lobster as much as the next person, but when I travel somewhere to experience a natural environment, I just can't seem to coalesce in my mind the raw, natural, earthy pleasure of a daylong hike with the erudite pleasures of fine dining. I can't drive in air-conditioned comfort to a major geologic formation and be happy with a photo taken through a car window. Yet increasingly it seems that more and more people are satisfied with seeing less and less; that too many people believe all the comforts of home can be integrated into an outdoor experience.

I remember the first time I came back from a hike in the Funeral Mountains and stood high atop an eroded butte looking down upon the lot full of trailers at Furnace Creek. Back then I was hiking and climbing and crawling around the Death Valley region on a regular basis and was frequently approached by kind, older couples who were intent upon "taking me in" for the night. "You don't want to sleep out there on the ground," they would tell me. "Come on in and get comfortable." And so I would be ushered through the screen door of their Winnebago or Airstream and into a climate-controlled environment complete with shag carpeting, color TV, hot and cold running water, comfy beds, and the aromas of home cooking and portable toilet freshener. On these occasions, I would pay a short visit, have a glass of lemonade, compliment them on their decorating, thank them for inviting me in, then escape as fast as possible to my campsite, glad to be out in the open air again.

Nothing much has changed, I'm afraid. If anything, the Winnebago people bring *more* conveniences with them these days. Instead of toaster ovens, their trailers now sport microwaves. Television sets are supplemented by rooftop satellite dishes, and cell phones are an integral part of some folks' communal experiences with nature.

Why do so many people who travel to spectacular natural environments like Death Valley feel the need to haul all these urban contrivances along with them? I believe it's because they want to feel as though they're back home, not out in the middle of nowhere. Home is comfortable; the desert is not. I can think of no other reason why tens of thousands of them pull into this gargantuan parking lot each year and extend their portable awnings, set out their Rubbermaid welcome mats, and hammer their roadrunner whirligigs into the rockhard desert pavement that William Lewis Manly and company trudged across a century and a half ago. Why do they bring those televisions and microwaves and boom boxes? Why do they flock to nearby concession outlets to buy fans and dark glasses and hats and sunscreen and iced tea and Pepsi and Danielle Steele paperbacks? Might it be that they love the desert, but only on their own suburban terms? Might it be that they are happy to visit Death Valley, but only if they can avoid feeling hot, dusty, sweaty, scratchy, thirsty, wary, or terrified? And yet, aren't these the sorts of sensations that a trip to the desert should be all about?

If we think of Death Valley National Park as a living, breathing thing—not unlike a human body—then its roads would constitute its circulatory system. If we could travel through the body's system of veins and arteries, we would eventually visit all the major organs: the heart, brain, liver, lungs, kidneys, and so on. Likewise, one who travels each and every paved road in Death Valley will eventually see all the major attractions—at least those that have been linked by these highways and pointed out on maps and travel guides as most worth seeing.

Unfortunately, cruising along the main roads in Death Valley will take you only to those places marked in bold on the map and deemed to be representative of the region as a whole. But in Death Valley, as in all national parks and monuments, state highways will always pass by thousands of other locales that might be of great interest but haven't been set up to accommodate visitors or are just too far from the main road.

And while the blacktop arteries may speed you along efficiently, they will not allow you to experience the enigmatic ambience of a night in a miner's shack atop a windy bluff in the Panamints. They won't expose you to the soulful silence of a solitary trek through the upper reaches of a slot canyon high in the Grapevine Mountains. They won't encourage you to use all your senses to their fullest in exploring all that this marvelously vast and empty place has to offer. In short, they will not lead you to the spirit or soul of this living entity called Death Valley.

But if you leave the paved roads for just an hour or so, you can sample at least a small taste of the real Death Valley, the place as it must have looked to members of the Bennett-Arcane party, or as the first single-blanket prospectors might have viewed it, or as the borax miners working out in the saline belly of the place must have experienced it.

Even if you're driving a low-clearance suburban sedan, you can turn off the main highway and take the bouncy, dusty, teeth-chattering dirt track up and into the Marble and Cottonwood Canyons complex. And what will you miss if you don't see this place? You won't experience the environment of a desert canyon ecosystem with massive cottonwood trees lining a boulder-strewn streambed that flows with sparkling clear water much of the year. You won't see mule deer or coyotes or jackrabbits or chuckwallas. You won't see the secluded worlds of desert greenery that are so often hidden behind cliffs of rock, up boulder-strewn alluvial fans, and around the bends of high-walled arroyos.

If you travel only along paved roads, the end of the line in northern Death Valley will be Ubehebe Crater. But if you are brave enough to leave Ubehebe behind and travel twenty-eight miles on a rough but romantic road across a red and black volcanic landscape, you will pass through a Joshua tree forest and into a hidden little valley where the bizarre and beautiful Racetrack dry lake glimmers in the sun. There you will encounter the still unsolved mystery of the moving rocks and have the opportunity to experience the insignificance of man and the grand scale of nature by standing alone in the middle of a vast dry playa bed.

Or you might opt to visit the secretive Eureka Valley with its singing sand dunes and endangered evening primrose plants. This isolated spot is reached via a series of dirt and crushed rock roads—a trip of either forty or fifty-one miles from the nearest highway, depending on which way you approach it. It may take you three hours or more, but you will have experienced one of the most beautiful desert valleys and seen one of the tallest sand dune systems in the nation.

Rather than traveling south from Furnace Creek along State Highway 178, take the cutoff about six miles south that takes you across the Devil's Golf Course and over to the West Side Road, a dusty track that parallels the eastern base of the Panamints and passes by a number of tepid springs where the '49ers satisfied their thirst more than 150 years ago. Visit the site of the Eagle Borax Works, first borax operation on the valley floor. Owner Isadore Daunet killed himself in 1882 after two years of operation proved unsuccessful because the borax solutions wouldn't crystallize in the intense heat of summer. A bit farther down the road, rest a while at Bennett's Long Camp, possibly the last stop for the Bennett-Arcane party before they escaped the valley with their rescuers, John Rogers and William Lewis Manly. If you listen carefully, you might hear echoes of Asabel Bennett calling, "The boys have come, the boys have come!"

If you own a high-clearance four-wheel-drive vehicle or can beg, borrow, or steal one, your options for a true desert wilderness experience are multiplied by a hundred or more. Travel to the extreme northeast corner of the park and take the bone-jarring twenty-mile drive from Rhyolite to the solitude of Phinney Canyon. Cutting through hills clothed in piñon pine and juniper, the canyon offers mining ruins, a small seep spring where mule deer gather, and a dramatic view from the crest of the Grapevine Mountains to Death Valley below and the peaks of the Sierras in the distance. Or take the Echo Canyon Road to visit the ghost town of Schwaub, see a natural window of rock called the Eye of the Needle, and climb a limestone staircase to the crest of the Funeral Mountains.

If you have most of a full day available, take a trek up the steep and rugged Johnson Canyon Road to the site of an unusual agricultural enterprise in the western foothills of the Panamints. During the heyday of Panamint City, some enterprising Swiss orchardists began growing vegetables for sale to miners. With the proceeds, they enlarged their operation to include fruit and nut trees, but Panamint City was already a near ghost town by the time their first crop was harvested. After the Swiss departed, there arrived a Shoshone chief of great girth and good humor, named Hungry Bill, who filed a homestead and settled here. It takes a short hike to reach the ranch site from the end of the road, but the chance of eating a fresh peach makes it worth the effort.

All these experiences, times a hundred, can be encountered by anyone willing to stray off the well-traveled roads and expend several hours in pursuit of less accessible objectives. But there is yet one further step that can be taken to move beyond the visitation of place to the experience of environment. The soul of Death Valley is found in the true wilderness experiences that can be obtained only by leaving your vehicles aside and hiking to places that might see only a handful of people in any given year.

Trek north from the mouth of Titus Canyon for less than a mile and enter the magnificent narrows of Fall Canyon to follow the twisting gap as it climbs its way into the Grapevine Range. Or hike a few miles farther and experience the bright glow of sun on stone in Red Wall Canyon.

Hike across the salt flats from Ashford Mill and climb the sloping sides of Shore Line Butte. Spend a day at Saline Valley Marsh and see how many of its 124 species of birds you can spot. Scramble down through the mysterious narrows of Bighorn Gulch. See where Frenchman Jean Lemoigne settled and dug his silver mine after his friend Isadore Daunet committed suicide. Hike to the crest of Telescope Peak where, standing among the ancient bristlecone pines, you can look to the east and see Badwater, lowest point in the western hemisphere, or look to the west and see Mount Whitney, highest point in the contiguous United States.

Leave the highways and dirt roads and jeep trails and hiking tracks behind and set out on foot to visit places like Last Chance Mountain, Dry Bone Canyon, Mormon Point, Funeral Peak, Hooligan Mine, Corkscrew Peak, Coffin Canyon, Lost Wash, and Virgin Spring. It is at these alternately shaded, windswept, rock-strewn, sunburnt, ghostly, stark, subtle, and glaring places that you will sense the soul of this place beginning to materialize. Here that you will know you have felt the spirit of Death Valley pass through you. Here where you will have at last left behind the modern world and stepped foot, however briefly, into the nineteenth century, the Precambrian era, the ice age, or any of a thousand other historical and prehistoric times.

Then again, if you'd really rather, you can drive down the highway from Furnace Creek to see Mushroom Rock—what's left of it, at any rate. In 1983 a large chunk of the formation at last crumbled to the ground, altering its appearance from that of a broccoli floweret to something more closely resembling a melted satellite dish. In a manner most uncharacteristic of the federal government, the authorities have yet to erect a sign at the site stating when the wayward chunk will be reattached to the mother rock.

Salvation

NOW THAT WILLIAM LEWIS MANLY and John Rogers have at last returned to the bitter little camp on the floor of the valley, all are anxious to know the nature of the road that lies before them. Manly does his best to sound hopeful, but candidly tells the others that only by the grace of God have he and Rogers returned at all. As they listen, he tells of deep snow in the great mountains to the north of their trail. He talks of black and desolate ranges to the south. He describes the vast dry plains beyond.

And yet Manly shares hopeful news as well. Sally and Abigail beam when he describes the view from the top of a low hill that finally marked his arrival in hospitable territory. From this vantage point, he and Rogers spied a herd of fat cattle and acres of green meadowland as far as the eye could see. Less than a mile in the distance was a Spanish ranch where they would soon be nursed back to health. By an odd stroke of fate, Manly had sprained his leg just days before reaching the little rancho. The two had originally planned to go on to the coast but changed their minds when their Spanish hosts insisted on giving them shelter and fetching a doctor to care for Manly. It was while they were here that they met a man named French, a rancher of some repute in the region, who gave them a good packsaddle and two horses to make the return trip.

"In a way," says Manly, "my bunged up leg was a blessing to us all, for we were able to head back here again just a few days later, more refreshed than ever and equipped with two horses and our little one-eyed mule."

"But I see no horses," says Asabel Bennett.

Manly drops his eyes. "We had to leave them behind," he says sadly. "They couldn't scale the walls of the canyon and we had to leave them at the base of a dry fall. I suspect they're up in that canyon yet."

"But little one-eye here climbed the walls like an alley cat," says Rogers, "and he carried what vittles we weren't obliged to eat ourselves."

He retrieves a pack from the back of the sorrowful little animal and begins pulling out the paltry supply of remaining goods. It seems like a feast to the others—flour and beans, good dried meat with fat still clinging to it, and assorted other goods that the Spanish ranchers were kind enough to send with them.

Asabel and Jean now share their experiences with Manly and Rogers, starting with the slow but steady desertion by many parties in camp. When Asabel mentions the departure of Captain Culverwell, Manly glances first at Rogers, then tells the others, "The captain's body lies in the sand not five miles south of here."

"His tracks turn right around at a spot where somebody made camp," adds Rogers.

"It must've been the Wades' camp," says Jean, "because they headed south not two hours before Culverwell decided to leave."

"If so," says Manly, "then I fear the Wades have perished too, since the desert to the south drops even lower in elevation. The desert to the south looks to be an evil place, far drier and hotter than our present campsite."

Jean Arcane shakes his head sadly. "If only they had remained here in camp with us," he says quietly.

"Their only hope would have been to head west through the mountains as John and I did," says Manly, "though it would have meant leaving their wagon behind."

"Better to lose a damn wagon than your life," says Rogers.

It is well after midnight before anyone can sleep, but at last the returning heroes turn their little mule out to graze and pile into bed, exhausted from their long trek. Both are delighted to have sheets and blankets for the first time in nearly a month.

At first light, all are up early. After dressing, Manly and Rogers walk over to the oxen and start checking their hooves.

"As raggedy as they are," says Rogers, "they're a far sight better'n when we left 'em here."

As they ready the beasts and begin packing the remaining provisions, Asabel approaches the two.

"Is there any reason we can't just climb out of here the same way you came down?" he asks.

"It's possible," says Rogers. "Only problem is the dry falls. They'll be on the downhill side now and they're pretty straight up and down with no ledges to speak of for animals to use. Little one-eye here made out all right, but I don't know if the oxen could manage."

"We haven't much choice," says Jean, "especially since you know this route offers water. Perhaps we can come up with some way to drop the oxen down and over the falls."

Manly still appears worried. "I've been thinking about the children," he says at last. "Whatever route we choose, it will be a lengthy hike. How will they manage such a long walk?"

Asabel Bennett smiles, his first in a long time.

"There's a problem we all thought about ourselves," he says.

He walks over to his wagon, where Jean Arcane's boy, three-year-old Charley, sits in the sand next to little Martha Bennett.

"If I might borrow your boy for a minute," Asabel tells Jean, "I'll show Lewis here how we plan to accommodate our little ones."

Bending down, he scoops up Charley and tucks him under his arms before strolling over to the oxen.

Lifting the toddler into the air, Asabel plops him down in one of the saddlebags that hang over the broad back of Old Crump. Charley settles in comfortably, then begins rocking as though about to gallop off.

Manly pulls off his hat and scratches his head. "I'll be damned," he exclaims, even though he is not generally prone to swearing.

"What I want to know," says Rogers, "is where you got those saddlebags."

"Jean and I took two strong hickory shirts, turned the sleeves inside out, sewed up the necks, then stitched the shirts together by the tail," explains Asabel. "You'll have to admit they make dandy pockets for the children."

"As for George and Melissa," puts in Jean, "we figure they're old enough to cling to Old Crump's back with the help of a blanket round his belly."

"As long as Old Crump goes smooth and steady and don't decide to kick up and scatter things," says Rogers, "I 'spect your plan will work."

In short order, they are off, the children sitting comfortably atop Old Crump and the two women riding atop their own oxen. The rest walk alongside leading the other three oxen, with Rogers in the lead, followed by Asabel, Jean, and Manly in the rear.

After hiking south about a mile, Manly points to a broad wash leading up into the mountains.

"This is the place," he says. "We head up this canyon and in two nights we'll be at the same water holes that so refreshed John and me on our way back to get you."

Things begin smoothly enough and little Martha Bennett and Charley Arcane seem to enjoy the trip for a while, even going to sleep now and then. But before long, the way grows rough and they tire of being jostled about as the oxen trudge up the rocky wash. George and Melissa leave their perch in short order, preferring to pick their way among the sharp-edged rocks and small boulders rather than abuse their backsides. Not long after, the little ones begin to cry and complain. After listening for a few hours to these pitiful cries, Jean Arcane throws down his double-barrel rifle and says, "I have no more use for you." Then he walks over to Old Crump, pulls his little boy out of the saddlebag, and gives him a great big hug in the bargain.

"From now on," he says, "I'll carry you instead of that gun. I'll carry you until I drop if need be, because you've never asked for any of this, and my son deserves as much comfort as I can make him."

As she watches her husband, Abigail Arcane wipes at her eyes and beams with love for the man who so loves his little son.

Asabel Bennett then follows suit, lifting Martha from her saddlebag, which makes the little one quite happy. Even Old Crump seems pleased to be relieved of his passengers. As they continue up the canyon, Manly and Rogers decide to go ahead and set up a camp. When the ragtag party reaches that camp after several hours, both Sally and Abigail are grateful to see the blankets that have been spread on the ground for them. They fairly dive for these blankets and just lie there while the rest set to unloading what they'll need for the night.

By this time the women have begun to complain of sore feet and broken skin on their heels. While the men do their best to cheer them up, Sally and Abigail sit on their blankets in their wrinkled dresses with uncombed hair and swollen eyes. The women are the perfect pictures of dejection and it soon becomes clear that their swollen feet and stiff joints have left them entirely unprepared for the number of miles ahead.

"I'm afraid for the women," confides Manly to the other men. "We've already endured two dry camps in a row. To reach the water holes near the top of this range, we will need the better part of a day's travel. I don't believe they can make it in their present state."

"It's true, Lewis," says Rogers. "They're looking poorly all right."

"I'm inclined to let Sally and Abigail rest a while longer," says Manly. "The wait will be worth it if their condition improves."

"I trust there will be no harm in our praying, gentlemen."

"For a miracle?" asks Jean.

"For one last chance," says Manly. "For hope and luck and a second wind for the ladies."

As the women rest, the men hike up a craggy ridgeline about three or four hundred yards from camp. From here they seek a view of the distance they have yet to travel. Far ahead, the slope to the east is met by the same ridge they stand atop; between this and the main mountain is another gentle slope scattered over with sagebrush and what appears to be stools of bunchgrass here and there between. The place where they stand is slightly lower than the mountains either north or south, which appear craggy and difficult to climb. The view from the backbone of this ridge is clear enough for them to see in almost every direction. To the west and south the land seems fairly level, with a half-dozen dark and barren buttes rising from the plain. Manly points out the route they will follow, noting prominent landmarks and tracing a path with his finger for what the others figure to be about 125 miles.

"It will be a long journey, friends, but we'll make it; of that I'm certain. We've come too far to give up and we all must take heart in the fact that we are out of that cursed sink at last, and onto higher ground."

"Thanks be to God for that," says Asabel. "I won't mind being the first to say 'Good-bye, Death Valley.'"

Turning to face west again, the men scramble down the slope of the steep ridge, each saying a prayer that the women will be rested and ready to continue. Once back in camp, they are pleased to see that the morning sun has warmed the women's spirits along with their tired muscles. They are moving about the camp and have fed the children and started to ready themselves for travel. Just as the men view this hopeful scene, a cool and tonic breeze blows down from the snowy peak to the south. It seems the very thing to brace them for the journey ahead.

"The Lord has sent us a sign," says Manly. "A cooling breeze from heaven above."

"We're ready to travel," says Sally Bennett. "I'm thirsty and want to reach those springs just as soon as we can."

"Then ladies, gentlemen," says Manly, "I suggest we be on our way."

Three weeks later, the remnants of the Bennett-Arcane party at last come in sight of the low hills that Manly claims separate the desert from the fertile valleys of California. This green and grassy land is still some seventy-five miles away, but they know that— God willing—it will be less than a week before they make their way out of this desert and into the promised land they have been seeking for more than a year.

The vegetation here ranges from small bushes and shrubs to some of the oddest looking trees they have ever seen. To Manly, they appear much like the sort of tree a child might draw, with one main trunk and three or four bare limbs thrusting out in all directions, each topped by a wad of pointy, dagger-shaped leaves. They will later learn that the Spanish call these yuccas, but Manly takes to calling them cabbage trees, and the name sticks with the others.

For three days they cross this strange desert landscape, crowded with cabbage trees and spiny cactus and occasional piles of huge, creamy white boulders that appear to have been tossed out here by whom and when and in what sort of humor they don't know. Then, on the fourth day, they at last reach the first gentle foothills of the range they must cross to reach the California valley.

They make camp that night near a half-dozen skulls of cattle that have been killed or have died. What might have been a depressing sight under any other circumstances is actually cause for celebration, for they know these are the remains of herd animals, not wild beasts. It seems likely that the animals wandered away from a Spanish ranch or might even have been stolen and herded out here by someone for their meat. Whatever the case, their bones tell the travelers that they are not far from hospitable country.

After a few more days of travel, they are forced to kill another ox for food, leaving them just four—Old Crump, Brigham, and two others without names. It is a sad occasion each time they have to butcher one of these loyal servants.

"I feel each time as though we are striking down a good friend," says Rogers as he helps Manly prepare the meat. "I honestly believe that if we could gain strength by eating sagebrush or by catching and eating those little horned lizards that dart around us all day, I would be more than happy to forgo ox meat without a single complaint."

But here they are, with no choice but to save themselves by killing the beasts that have labored for them so faithfully throughout their long journey.

After three more days of travel, they arrive late in the afternoon at the low rise of hills that Manly and Rogers had described to the others when they returned to rescue them. They all know what awaits them on the other side of that rise, and it is with a kind of reverence that they approach the slope and make the short hike to the top.

The view from the summit is every bit as rewarding as Lewis has related to them. Far below, a herd of fat, multicolored cattle grazes on the greenest grass any of them have ever seen. A little creek meanders around this thousand-acre meadow, which is crisscrossed with a patchwork of wildflowers—reds and yellows and blues and whites. Here and there among the cattle are a number of sleek black horses, fit and beautiful to the eye. And in the distance, probably no more than a mile, is a little house made of mud that has dried to a grayish color. This is the same house where Manly and Rogers sought help after their long ordeal in the desert.

Taken as a whole from the top of the hill, the beautiful sight is altogether too much for Sally and Abigail. The two women slowly drop to their knees and bow their heads as if in church. They cry and kiss their children and cry some more. They pray a little and hug their husbands and then cry a while longer until they have pretty much drained their eyes dry. Finally they just sit there gazing down at that little valley as if it is the loveliest place on earth.

As they stand there, Manly comes over and tells the others that this day is March 7, by his calculation. Then he adds the year—1850—as though perhaps the others have lost track. He adds that this date and that of November 4, 1849, the day they took the ill-advised "shortcut," will be fixed in his mind forever. He also says something that seems a little out of character for Manly. He tells the others that if he ever gets hold of the man who showed them that cursed map of the shortcut or the man who drew the thing, he will take them out and skin the hides off both of them. Then he strolls on over to the women and sits down beside them to say a little prayer.

After more than four months of steady walking through the desert, the two hours they spend atop that hill are not without good reason. But Manly finally says that if they want to reach that little adobe house before sunset, they had best get moving. And so the others load up their belongings again and start on down into the beautiful valley, the women each carrying a fine staff that Rogers has cut for them, and George and Melissa romping ahead and tumbling down the grassy slope with a lot of giggling and shrieking and silliness. Had anyone seen them strolling down the hill that day, they might have guessed they were only coming back from a daylong family outing.

In truth, they have been traveling for months through unforgiving country. But their journey is now at an end, their salvation at hand, and their collective nightmare at long last over.

CHAPTER THIRTEEN

※

THE SOLITUDE OF SIMPLE SOULS

*Man can will nothing unless he has first understood that he must
count on no one but himself; that he is alone, abandoned on earth . . .
without help, with no other aim than the one he sets himself, with no
other destiny than the one he forges for himself on earth.*

—JEAN PAUL SARTRE,
Being and Nothingness, 1943

Desert dawn. The first dull rays of the sun have risen above
the salt flats and begun to warm Death Valley's crusty
hide. But as the gargantuan trench awakens, its little brother
to the west, Panamint Valley, still slumbers in the shadow of
Telescope Peak.

Down in Panamint Valley, the dust from the previous day
has settled, the dunes of sand have cooled. At this early hour,

the dimly lit depression masquerades as an apparition, a slim shadow of its imposing relation to the east. Claiming neither notoriety nor traffic, the valley rests in peace with only the moonlight to reveal its existence.

Near the center of Panamint Valley stand a half-dozen crumbling adobe walls, all that remains of Ballarat, a mining supply town that boomed around the turn of the twentieth century. In its glory days Ballarat was home base to thousands of miners who worked nearby claims with names like Gold Bug and World Beater, Honolulu and Hemlock. Today the ghost town continues to be a sort of base camp—a jumping-off place for a small number of hikers, packers, and off-road drivers who come to explore the ruins of these same hard-rock operations. Within a handful of miles in any direction of Ballarat lie dozens of narrow dirt tracks that will rattle you up to such isolated spots as Goler Wash, Butte Valley, Jackpot Canyon, and Mormon Gulch.

At Indian Ranch, just a few miles north of Ballarat's crumbling walls, squats a row of dented trailers, a few slouching storage sheds, a smattering of old car bodies in various stages of decay, and a nondescript cement block building that houses a bar. Running the place in the early '70s was a skinny old gal named Stella, who sold the iciest cans of Coors to ever touch my lips. In my mind, her birdlike frame still perches atop the black and gold Naugahyde cushion of a bar stool as she keeps watch over the dim confines of her smoky domain. Stella's kingdom consisted of a half-dozen orange Formica tables, a row of collectible bourbon bottles, a dented jukebox crooning "Please Release Me," and two aged pool tables whose green felt surfaces were crisscrossed by ragged scars of gray duct tape.

I can't claim any great powers of recollection for having preserved these images so clearly in my mind; it's simply the only way I ever saw her—seated at the bar with one bony hand dangling an ash-laden Marlboro over the dingy linoleum while the other caressed a glass of whiskey-and-water the color of old newspapers. The first time I set foot in the place, two big dogs lay peacefully at Stella's feet, their dusty coats embedded with brittlebush burrs and one of them sporting a long black smudge he'd received from dragging himself under one of the deceased automobiles outside. Although I would pass through the door of this dim little establishment a dozen more times over the next few years, I never saw those two dogs in any state other than sound asleep, one resting his square-jawed head atop the other's rising and falling stomach and both snoring so loud they could be heard above the whine of the generator that ran the Pepsi cooler behind the bar. A third dog, some sort of shorthaired hunting breed, could generally be found just inside the front door, its stub of a tail wagging uncertainly and its four large paws anchored to the floor as if nailed there. I remember being put off the first time I glanced down at this animal and saw the worms dropping from his anus like meat from a grinder.

Stella's mind was a storehouse of news and gossip about activities in Panamint Valley and the surrounding region. She never failed to inform me how many worthless mines were being worked or which patrons had gotten shit-faced and sliced each other up with broken bottles. She could tell you the name of the beer truck driver who was "poking" the wife of a Trona tavern owner. And she always knew the tiniest details of any half-baked decisions the "assholes" at the state highway department had made. Only occasionally would she pause to punctuate her acid commentary with a smoke-laced, three-pack-a-day chuckle, a quick drag on her Marlboro, and a little sip of whiskey.

Stella was a woman alone in a world of hard-rock miners, long-haul truckers, drunk-ass Indians, drugged-out hippies, and the handful of tourists from L.A. who would now and again drift off the main road and arrive at her bar frantically searching for civilization. Stella's sacred mission in life—one she pursued with unrelenting devotion—was to observe all that went on about her, store it in her mind, then play it back to those who were willing to sit and listen. Looking back, I often wish I'd listened more intently; that I'd asked her more questions. But what captured my interest in those formative years was anything but Stella's character studies or personal essays on the failings of government drones. I was, instead, seduced by the hard-edged history of Panamint Valley—a territory whose repute was built atop a foundation of stage robberies and gunfights, velvet brothels and golden cliffs, Chinese laborers and lost mines, flash floods and unnamed washes littered with the bones of unknown men. Consequently I corralled much of what she told me in some deep crevice of my mind where the information promptly withered and died like a hobbled horse in a box canyon. Perhaps one day I'll head in there to retrieve the mummified remains.

Fortunately there were other bright nuggets that stayed with me—bits of lore and local history that glimmered enticingly and lured me, over the years that followed, to places I might never have known about had I not parked my ass on a bar stool and spent an hour sipping Coors and nodding my head. One of these secret places was the camp of Ballarat saloon owner Chris Wicht.

I use the word "secret" in the sense that this was a special place, not that I had learned about some sequestered spot to which no other living beings had ever traveled or could have discovered for themselves. Hundreds had bounced their way up the alluvial apron to Surprise Canyon long before I did and hundreds more would do so long after my first bone-jarring trip was over. Fact is, anyone who walks, rides, or drives the twelve or thirteen miles to Panamint City passes right by Chris's campsite about a mile inside the canyon's narrow walls. But few stop here anymore. There's hardly reason to, now that the last crumbling walls of the cabin have been reduced to slivers of wood and chunks of rock; now that the hinges and latches from its doors and windows have been hauled away by memento collectors; now that the shallow pond of spring water has leaked its contents and been choked by weeds. There is, in fact, little left today at the site but the broad canopy of cottonwood branches that once shaded a roof but now cast their shadows over the nearly invisible outline of a stone foundation.

But Chris Wicht lived there all right, from 1902 to nearly 1920, the same years that Ballarat thrived, and his establishment was the favorite watering hole in Panamint Valley. It also was the most dangerous. Long before the China Lake Naval Weapons Center was created to the southwest, the Ballarat saloon was the preferred place for weapons testing. And Chris did not escape the usual assortment of perils that have long been synonymous with bartending. Two or three times a month he would find himself riding slowly up the winding trail from Ballarat to his cabin with painful injuries only a bartender could love. One night it might be a bleeding gash from a knife wound, sterilized with whiskey and wrapped with muslin for the trip home. Another day might end with one cheek bruised and swollen, courtesy of a whiskey-filled projectile. The following night Chris might leave the saloon with his right hip smarting from a bullet that grazed him on the way toward some luckless miner who stupidly tried to cheat at faro.

Despite what modern-day thrill seekers might conclude, Chris Wicht did not come to Ballarat for the excitement. In his mind, the risk of bodily harm was no more, no less than an acceptable trade-off for comfort—the comfort of four walls and a roof to keep him out of the sun and rain and blowing sand. Tending bar also produced the first steady income he'd ever realized, a flow of cash considerably more rewarding than the pittance he'd earned as a borax miner on the floor of Death Valley. That job had carried its own costs in the forms of boredom, heat exhaustion, and muscle fatigue.

By the mid-1890s, several large-scale borax companies were operating in and around Death Valley, some employing dozens of men at a single alkaline marsh. But the mining process was still pretty much a solitary endeavor. Each workday, Chris and the other miners would head out into the marshes with their shovels, searching for the heaviest deposits of borax in the thick saline soup. Whenever they spotted a promising concentration of powder, they would scrape the material off the surface and load it into buckets. These would later be dumped into iron water tanks that were heated up to boil away impurities and crystallize the material. The crystallized borax was carried by twenty-mule-team wagons or railroad, depending on the mining site, to Mojave, Boron, and other desert stations, then to Southern California refineries to be converted into a host of household and industrial products.

When Chris and the other miners weren't immersed in this creative and fulfilling occupation, they spent their free time sleeping in dugouts, simple holes cut into banks of earth—holes that had the nasty habit of caving in on their occupants. But for the most part, theirs was a life of labor, liquor, lassitude, and loneliness.

It does not appear, however, that loneliness was a major concern for Chris Wicht. In many ways he actually chose solitude, a fact explaining why he might have chosen to be a borax miner; why he might have become the bartender at Ballarat and elected to leave the saloon each night and ride on horseback some six miles up a narrow, twisting, frequently washed-out road to the secluded cabin he called home. Adding to that seclusion, Chris's place was located up inside the canyon's narrow walls at a point where a series of bends in the road cut off all views down to the canyon's mouth. In the other direction, an angular slab of slickrock lifted the canyon floor and turned it abruptly to the right, obscuring any views in this direction. There is still no horizon here, still no sunrise or sunset. To see the sky, you need to look straight up.

Late one spring I made the decision to spend a night at Chris's old homestead, perhaps to better understand what he might have experienced living there in seclusion between those precipitous canyon walls. The weather was warm that afternoon as I departed Indian Ranch and headed south along the base of the mountains toward the turnoff marked "Panamint City" on a small piece of wood nailed to a post.

After clattering up the rocky alluvium for about three miles, I reached the mouth of the canyon, pulled to a stop, and got out to switch the hubs to four-wheel drive. Then I stood there a minute and gazed back down at the road I'd just taken, the dust from my wheels still suspended above its surface. A thousand feet below me and four miles to the south lay Ballarat's plaintive ruins, while the rotting cars and dented trailers of Indian Ranch huddled a few miles off to the north. Far across the valley, the razorback peaks of the Sierras were just visible above the low rise of Maturango Peak, highest point in the Argus Range, which separates the Panamint and Owens Valleys.

Bidding a silent farewell to my last view of civilization, I climbed back in my rig, shifted into low, and started on up the hardscrabble canyon floor. Clambering over sandwiched layers of bedrock, I climbed another thousand feet in just under two miles, finally arriving at the hallowed site of Chris Wicht's camp. Here a faint track left the main wash and climbed up to a little shelf of rock that hugged the south wall and hung there above the canyon floor. In the waning light of early evening, I chose a spot by the massive trunk of a cottonwood tree and set up camp—which is to say I threw my sleeping bag down on the ground. Nearby lay the cool but shallow pond that Chris had used to get his water; I promptly christened a twelve-pack of Buckhorn beneath its placid surface.

Chris, it must be understood, was an alcoholic. And though he lived to see his eightieth birthday, it was drink that eventually killed him, not a knife or bullet wound. Some have gone so far as to say that the alcohol helped fend off infection all those years and may have actually prolonged his life. Whatever the case, it seemed only proper to me at the time that I should experience my night at his camp through the same veil of unreality he must himself have worn for viewing life. And so, after toasting my host and downing a brew, I quickly disposed of a can of cold stew, lay back on my bag, and awaited the solitude.

To spend any time at all in this place is to believe you are the only person left in the world. In some respects it's probably more secluded today than a century ago. It certainly seemed that way when I made camp up there those many years ago. Instead of a bustling supply town six miles down the alluvial fan, Ballarat was nothing more than a few rows of crumbling walls. Down at Indian Ranch there was Stella, a few tipsy patrons, and the smell of stale beer. And up at Panamint City, five more miles up-canyon, the only residents were a handful of shell-shocked vets and burnt-out hippies occupying the few remaining miners' shacks.

Panamint City had once been a wild and woolly silver mining camp with a population of two thousand miners and a standing record of fifty fatal shootings in the first four years the town boomed. So violent was Panamint's reputation that the Wells Fargo Company refused to freight its ore down Surprise Canyon for fear of ambush in the canyon's tortuous narrows. This didn't stop the town's mine owners, however. They merely changed the way they cast the silver—molding it into ponderous quarter-ton balls—and freighted the unwieldy loads down-canyon in open wagons without further incident.

By the time darkness enveloped the canyon, I had killed five cans of beer and recycled three. I had allowed my fire to die down and was lying atop my bag preparing to doze off, but I remember being quite wide awake and strangely sensitive to the sounds around me. One of these was the persistent clicking of an obscure little bird whose exact location and species escaped me. After a while the local crickets joined in; then I began to hear a rustling in the uppermost branches of the cottonwood. It seemed an odd noise because there was no breeze that night. Then from some distance up-canyon came the trickling melody of running water. I knew it to be the tiny flow that bubbles up from Limekiln Spring, travels down a short stretch of exposed bedrock, then disappears back into the sand.

Of course, all these sounds were merely the ordinary music a person expects to hear at night in a desert canyon. It was only after I had relieved myself for the fourth time and returned to my bag that I noticed a less natural, more disturbing sound—that of feet shuffling along the rocky wash somewhere up-canyon, maybe fifty yards away. Although my senses had deteriorated by this time into a less than responsive mode, I did manage to rise up on one elbow so I could hear better. I also became suddenly conscious of a comment Stella had made that afternoon, something about the spirit of Chris Wicht being spotted now and again hovering about his camp. But she had grinned when she said it. And, besides, dead men don't shuffle.

As I continued to listen, the sound of footsteps kept up for a while, then stopped, as if whoever made them had paused to consider which way to go. It made perfect sense; if someone had just rounded the bend in the canyon above and stood now in the middle of the wash, he or she now had the option of continuing down toward the canyon's mouth or veering left and following the little path up to Chris's camp, where I lay as still as I could, trying hard not to piss in my pants. Their choice at last made, the footsteps resumed their journey, clattering across the loose shale path that climbed above the canyon floor and led to the little outcropping I now occupied.

I should mention that this was not a particularly great place to be alone at night and hear the sound of approaching footsteps. A few years earlier and just a few miles south of Chris's camp, the twisted innards of Goler Wash had been the stomping ground of Charles Manson and company. When they weren't hacking apart state-owned picnic tables or destroying highway signs, they had been diligently searching the Death Valley region for a vortex to the netherworld. And they had been hatching plans for a helter-skelter night of murder in the Los Angeles foothills. Though Manson had since been safely placed behind bars, he hadn't been the region's only colorful character; a number of other interesting personalities had reportedly claimed their own little patches of ground near Panamint Valley over the past few years. It just might be that the owner of the footsteps was a grizzled desert madman coming to reclaim what he considered his private property.

As I waited tensely, the crickets suddenly went quiet and a figure appeared from out of the darkness, a gray form that shuffled over to within a few inches of my sleeping bag, bent down, and struck a match just above my head. A second later, the hand in front of my nose shook the match out.

"Sorry, man," came a slurry voice. "Just seein' if you was alive."

"So far, so good," I think was my answer.

His words, entwined with the pungent aroma of homegrown weed, reassured me somewhat that the two of us were about equally wasted. This lessened my concerns that he would get the drop on me, though I still kept my guard as I struggled to sit up. But my nighttime visitor seemed less interested in hassling me than relieving himself of his bulging duffel bag, which he pulled from his shoulders and let drop to the ground before plopping down cross-legged alongside it. Then he fumbled in his shirt pocket and retrieved another joint.

"So," I stammered after managing to rise, "you live around here?"

For a moment, I wondered if my question had sounded as stupid to him as it had to me, but he offered no response. He was too busy drawing deeply on his joint while gazing up at the slit of night sky above us.

By now the film over my eyes had cleared enough for me to glimpse a face in the glow of the joint. He looked to be your standard hippie—bearded, unkempt, wild-eyed, faded bandanna, soiled denim jacket—and the reefer, of course. As I took all this in, it didn't take long for my fermented brain cells to panic again; I now began to wonder if Manson himself had escaped from prison and was returning to his former stomping ground to look up some old friends. At the very least, this might be his brother or cousin or real estate broker sent here to ferret out a new retreat. But after several minutes my guest had yet to discuss the local housing market or offer any signs of being the least bit insane. So I rose to my feet, moved a few yards away, and took a leak. This provided at least some physical relief and allowed me to put things in clearer perspective.

Shuffling over to the fire, I stirred the coals a little and threw on a few sticks. Then I returned to the stranger's side and asked if he wanted a beer.

"Nah," he said, blowing out a cloud of smoke. "I quit drinking a year ago. Thought I might have a problem."

As he exploded in a fit of coughing, I walked over to the little pool, fished out a Buckhorn, then moved over to sit across from him on a jutting ledge of rock.

"You from L.A.?" he asked. "You look like you're from L.A."

I wasn't sure if the remark was meant to be flattering or an insult, but I nodded yes and said, "For now, anyway. I just got out of school in Oregon and came south to look for work."

"Oregon's all right," he said with a grin. "Got a good piece of ass there once."

"I don't know," I said, shaking my head. "I hear the ladies are pretty spongy up north with all that rain."

He peeled his joint from his lips and laughed; I tilted back my can and drank.

"You live up in Panamint?" I asked him.

"Used to," he said. "Had to leave."

"Oh yeah? How come?"

He offered no further information, just tipped back his head for a moment and stared up at the sky.

"Here by yourself?" he asked me at last.

I nodded. "I came to see what real solitude was like."

"Oh yeah? Whatcha think so far?"

"Hard to tell. I'm not really alone anymore, am I?"

"Depends how you look at it," he said. "I mean, I might be sittin' here across from you and all, but you're still alone in your head."

"In my head?"

"Sure, man. We're all alone in our heads. Ain't nobody climbin' in *there* with you."

"Yeah, I see what you mean. But . . . what if I told you what I was thinking? I mean, wouldn't that be like letting you inside my head?"

"No way, man," he said, "cause the second you start telling me what you're thinking, another thought'll be hatching back there. Then, you'll probably start thinking about what you're gonna tell me next, then maybe your nose'll start itching. Then you'll have to stop thinking about what you were gonna tell me because now you gotta think about scratchin' yourself. See what I mean?

"I . . . think so."

"And then another thought'll pop into your brain—then another and another and another. Ad infinitum, man. No way you can keep up with your thoughts fast enough to pass 'em on. A person's lucky if he can share five percent of what he's thinking. Face it, man, you're alone in there with your thoughts. All by yourself. Every second of every minute of every hour the rest of your fuckin' life."

"Maybe you're right."

"Sure as shit I'm right." He took a long draw, coughed again, and dragged his sleeve across his mouth.

"Okay, so let's say I *can* be alone in my head," I pressed on. "That doesn't mean I still don't need to get away from everybody—*physically*, I mean—now and then."

"Away, like out of L.A., you mean? Sure, that's cool. I don't like a lot of people in my hair either. All's I'm telling you is I could be dropped in the middle of, say, New York City. Or, Chicago, you know? Crowds all around me, and they still couldn't get inside my head. You wanna know why? 'Cause that's my place, and there's a big fuckin' sign at the door that says, 'Hey You, Asshole—keep out!'"

The stranger's eyes were all pupil now as they bored into my skull. I nodded, but dropped my glance from his gaze.

"In here," he said, tapping his head with his index finger, "that's where you go to really be by yourself." Then he took another long drag of his joint and looked off into the darkness down-canyon.

My campsite friend did not stay long. He seemed wary of the silence around us, of the darkness that was everywhere. After another few minutes, he picked himself up and threw his camouflage duffel bag over one shoulder. Then he announced he had to move on and walked off into the darkness as I stared bleary-eyed after him. When he had gone, I returned to my bag and lay down, gazing up at the night sky. Not long after, I fell back to sleep and found myself perched at the bar in the Ballarat Saloon, trading jokes with Stella and dodging bullets with old Chris Wicht.

Years later I would come to admire Sartre's writings on isolation and revel in Wordworth's "inward eye which is the bliss of solitude." But they would never affect me quite the same as the mumblings of this scraggly stranger at Chris Wicht's camp. Though mouthed in meandering cannabis drawl, his words carried a certain grace and elegance. They offered a simplicity of truth that challenged my long-held notions of aloneness, of the need we all have for solitude and space in a close and crowded world. I now know that whatever else we may choose to believe about who we are and the lives we lead, we must at some point come to recognize that we are born alone, we die alone, and in between—though we wander amidst throngs of fellow humans—we all are similarly alone in our thoughts, in our minds, in our inner concepts of reality. Each of us alone knows the dreams and fears and nameless horrors and fleeting moments of ecstasy that pass through our minds. And though each of us may attempt to verbalize our thoughts to others, to express the shape of our mind's unseen landscape, in the end it remains a private enclave, a wilderness we must wander alone. And yet in some ways it is a place far more real than the world of air and light and pleasure and pain—a slab of bedrock far more reliable than the fragile crust on which we tiptoe about between life and death.

❧❅❆❅❧

I never mentioned my late-night visitor to friends or family when I returned home the following day. It seemed the sort of experience that was best stored safely in that private world of my mind, something for me to savor alone when I needed. Then about two weeks later a co-worker asked me where, exactly, I had camped in Panamint Valley. I told him I had stayed up in Surprise Canyon, and he grinned broadly and said, "I thought you might have."

Then he told me about something he'd seen in the newspaper—a small item about a Vietnam vet who'd been living up in Panamint City with a handful of other disgruntled outcasts until he and his friend Arnold (an M-1 rifle he carried with him at all times) had a bloody altercation with another resident of the ghost town. Arnold and the vet had won, while their victim had died of his wounds. This prompted the vet to escape the area and elude an Inyo County manhunt in the Panamint Mountains for ten days before at last turning himself in at a sheriff's substation.

"Who knows . . ." I recall my friend saying. "The timing sounds about right. For all you know, this guy might have been lurking around somewhere near where you were camping. Maybe even standing right over you with his piece, watching you while you slept. Pretty creepy, huh?"

"Yeah, creepy," I said, nodding.

For much of that day I played with the facts and wondered. It might have been someone else that night, maybe just some wanderer with a duffel bag. Might have been, and yet . . .

The Vietnam vet was eventually convicted of second-degree murder and sentenced to a good number of years in prison, years I'm sure he spent in the vast wilderness of his own mind, unshackled and wandering free.

Arnold was sold at a police auction a year or two later.

Postscript

AFTER SPLITTING FROM the Bennett-Arcane party in November 1849, the Jayhawkers entered Death Valley in late December, spending only a few days there before escaping on foot via Towne Pass and what is now known as Jayhawker Canyon. Thirteen of them perished before reaching civilization, though none of them died in Death Valley itself. For at least a dozen years following their ordeal, those who survived held reunions each February 4, commemorating the day in 1850 that they reached the green hills of San Francisquito Canyon.

Nearly everyone who made it out of the Mojave Desert alive, did so on foot. Of the thirty-seven wagons to leave the Sand Walking Company in Utah and take the ill-fated shortcut leading to Death Valley, just one of them, the wagon owned by the Wade family, actually reached the Los Angeles basin intact.

William Lewis Manly and John Rogers led the remaining members of the party 250 miles across the Mojave Desert in twenty-one grueling days until reaching safety at the San Fernando Mission.

An odd addendum to the experiences of the Bennett-Arcane party involves model family man Asabel Bennett, who after their ordeal moved to the San Francisco area with his wife, Sally, and their children. There they had a fourth child, and his wife died shortly after. We may never know if his experiences in Death Valley had left a mark on Bennett, but after his wife's death, he gave away the baby girl and left his three other children, then teenagers, to fend for themselves while he went to Cedar City, Utah, to run a general store.

When the store failed, Bennett returned to Southern California and, in 1861, journeyed with a man named Charles Alvord back to Death Valley, where rumors of a gold find were fueling interest by prospectors. On a brief hike by himself, Alvord collected some rocks and had them assayed back in Los Angeles. To his surprise, they were found to have a high gold content.

Bennett and Alvord returned to Death Valley a second time, but Alvord was unable to locate the place where he had found the rocks. Certain that Alvord was lying, Bennett and three or four other men left him to die on the saline flats of the Amargosa sink.

Manly then ran into Bennett in Los Angeles. When Manly heard what had happened to Alvord, he persuaded Bennett to return with him to Death Valley and try to rescue the abandoned man. Along with a man named Caesar Twitchell, Manly and Bennett returned to Death Valley and found Alvord very much alive, though growing short of supplies. Bennett and Twitchell agreed to return to Los Angeles for food and gear while Manly and Alvord waited in Death Valley. Once again, Bennett never returned, leaving the two to struggle back to Los Angeles again, as Manly had done a dozen years before. Manly and Bennett never met again.

Manly tried a number of occupations during his life, from mining to farming. He eventually settled in the San Jose area, where he lived to be well into his eighties. Back in the 1850s, while his Death Valley travails were fresh in his mind, he wrote a book on his ordeals and left the manuscript with some relatives to read. A fire in their house destroyed the manuscript, and it was not until 1894 that he decided to reconstruct his adventures and write the book again. *Death Valley in '49* remains a classic tale of his experiences.

Two final ironies. As many as one hundred pioneers may have stumbled into Death Valley during the winter of 1849 to 1850. Of these, only Captain Culverwell actually died in the valley itself. And not a single one of the Jayhawkers, whose impatience to reach the goldfields led them to abandon the families traveling beside them, ever found any gold.

BIBLIOGRAPHY OF SELECTED SOURCES

ABBEY, EDWARD. *Desert Solitaire: A Season in the Wilderness.*
New York: Ballantine Books, 1968.

———. *The Journey Home.* New York: E. P. Dutton, 1977.

BRIER, REV. JOHN WELLS. "The Argonauts of Death Valley."
Grizzly Bear Magazine, Vol. IX, No. 2 (June 1911).

CORLE, EDWIN. *Death Valley and the Creek Called Furnace.*
Los Angeles: Ward Ritchie Press, 1973.

CRONKHITE, DANIEL. *Recollections of a Young Desert Rat.* Verde,
NV: Sagebrush Press, 1972.

———. *Death Valley's Victims.* Morongo Valley, CA: Sagebrush Press,
1977.

EDWARDS, FRANK. *Flying Saucers—Serious Business.*
New York: Bantam Books, 1966.

FLINCHUM, ROBIN. "Anatomy of a Desert Flood."
Pahrump Valley Times (Pahrump, NV), August 2004.

FOGELSON, ROBERT M. *The Fragmented Metropolis—
Los Angeles, 1850–1930.* Cambridge, MA:
Harvard University Press, 1967.

LEE, BOURKE. *Death Valley Men.* New York:
The MacMillan Company, 1932.

LONG, MARGARET. *Shadow of the Arrow.* Caldwell, ID:
Caxton Printers, 1950.

MANLY, WILLIAM LEWIS. *Death Valley in '49*. 1st ed.
San Jose, CA: Pacific Tree & Vine Co., 1894.

PUTNAM, GEORGE. *Death Valley and its Country*. 1st ed.
New York: Duell, Sloan & Pierce, 1946.

SPEARS, JOHN R. *Illustrated Sketches of Death Valley*. 1st ed.
New York: Rand, McNally & Company, 1892.

STREET, FRANKLIN. *California in 1850*. Historical reprint.
New York: Arno Press, 1973.

WEIGHT, HAROLD O. *Lost Mines of Death Valley*.
Twentynine Palms, CA: The Calico Press, 1953.

WELLS, EVELYN, AND PETERSON, Harry C. *The '49ers*.
Garden City, NY: Doubleday & Company, 1949.

ACKNOWLEDGMENTS

I would like to thank some pretty incredible people I have been privileged to know during various stages of my life. Together, they helped me achieve my lifelong goal of writing and publishing my first book.

Doris Felix, my fifth-grade teacher, urged all of us to keep journals of our daily lives. I can't stress how important this exercise was for an aspiring writer. Eve Bunting, my first writing workshop teacher, helped her fledgling writers turn two-dimensional characters into living, breathing people. My college writing instructors, Ursula Hegi and John Keeble, stressed the importance of creating compelling word pictures to draw readers in and keep them reading until the last sentence of the last page.

I also am indebted to a few other highly regarded writers who took the time to read my manuscript, make suggestions and offer words of praise and encouragement. Among these authors are Pat McManus, Peter Matthiessen, and J. Maarten Troost.

As for Gary Luke and his company of talented people at Sasquatch Books, I continue to be in awe of the creative direction, practical advice, and patient support they have offered me throughout the publication process.

Lastly, I would have made no forward progress had it not been for the faith, steadfast support, and always cheerful encouragement of my wonderful literary agent, Laurie Abkemeier. She has truly been the best friend, adviser, and confidant a writer could ever want.

ABOUT THE AUTHOR

John Soennichsen was born in Los Angeles and was exposed at an early age to the Mojave Desert region that surrounds the Los Angeles basin. He first visited Death Valley at age thirteen and was immediately drawn to the stark yet compelling landscape of rock and alluvium, salt and sand. For nearly two decades, he traveled to and explored the region extensively by foot and four-wheel drive.

After two years at California State University at Fullerton, he transferred to the University of Oregon, where he received his bachelor of science in journalism. He has remained in the Pacific Northwest, living in Eugene, Portland, and the college town of Cheney, Washington. During the past twenty years, Soennichsen has written more than one hundred articles, essays, and short fiction that have been published in a variety of regional and national publications.

Soennichsen lives on a five-acre ranch with his wife and two teenage sons. His daughter is a recent graduate of Eastern Washington University, from which Soennichsen received an MFA in creative writing in 1997.